THE QUICK FIX

A Simple Process
For Positive Change

BRADLEY G. QUICK

T0370377

Order this book online at www.trafford.com
or email orders@trafford.com

Most Trafford titles are also available at major online book retailers.

© Copyright 2010 Bradely G. Quick. First published by Trafford 2008.
All rights reserved. No part of this publication may be reproduced, stored in a retrieval system,
or transmitted, in any form or by any means, electronic, mechanical, photocopying, recording,
or otherwise, without the written prior permission of the author.

Printed in Victoria, BC, Canada.

ISBN: 978-1-4251-6148-4 (sc)

*Our mission is to efficiently provide the world's finest, most comprehensive book publishing
service, enabling every author to experience success. To find out how to publish your book,
your way, and have it available worldwide, visit us online at www.trafford.com*

 www.trafford.com

North America & international
toll-free: 1 888 232 4444 (USA & Canada)
phone: 250 383 6864 ♦ fax: 812 355 4082

Thanks to:

My mother (Betty Roberts) and father (Blaine Quick) for loving, supporting and believing in me throughout the years and not giving up on me. Edward Kim for his brotherly love and support. My Grandmother (Juanita Morgan) for her love, prayers, strong will and wise humor. My aunts, uncles and cousins for their generous and unconditional love. Bill Evans, Russ Regan, Pete Zackary, Marilyn & Ed Toth and JP & Kathleen for their time, participation, and belief in this process and in me. Tom Oren and Greg Montealvo for their editing in the beginning and David Michael Smith for his editing of this finale product. The Oxford Group, Bill Wilson and Dr. Bob for sharing their experiences and leading the way for me. Special thanks to all those who have crossed my path, aided me, and shared with me on my journey of self-discovery and recovery. Especially, Frank Cherry, Jeff Pohn, and Don Maxwell whose patience and guidance showed me the way to better living, The Raging Bastards, Jeffery Maitles, Mike Lally, Donnie Burke and movie Mike who, in my time of pain, need, hopelessness and despair came into my life, wanting nothing, picked me up, saved my ass and gave me the tools to move on. Thanks to each and every one of you for your words, guidance, hospitality and, especially, your influences.

www.bradleyquick.com

www.AdriaticPark.com

Thanks to:

To The Reader

I wish you may soon realize all you've strived to achieve throughout your life and that all your plans and dreams become your new reality. I also wish that all those you know and love, and those you have yet to meet, benefit directly through your efforts and influence.

My hope for you, as your friend, is that you be closer than ever to finding your purpose, your niche in this evolutionary process we know as life.

My goal as your friend is to share my experience, and engage in laughter and emotion with you, to not reject, but to accept all you excitedly, or not so enthusiastically, wish to share with me.

I acknowledge we're both fully engaged in living and that is, more often times than not, all encompassing. I assure you, however, that when our paths do cross, and our universes once again engage, the pleasure will be mine.

At that time, I hope we may share freely our journey, our plans, our fears and our desires, and part more enlightened and inspired than before.

Sincerely,
Your friend,
Bradley G. Quick

www.bradleyquick.com

www.Samplepledat.com

To The Reader

I wish you may soon realize all you've strived to
achieve throughout your life and that all your plans
and dreams become your new reality. I also wish that
all that you know and love, and those you have yet
to meet, impart directly through your efforts and
influence.

My hope for you, as your friend, is that you be
closer than ever to finding your purpose, your niche
in this exploratory process we know as life.

My goal as your friend is to share my experiences
and engage on a higher and emotional with you, to not
recall but to recount of votes vitedly or not contribute
casually with it by share with me.

I acknowledge we're both fully engaged in living,
and that's, more often, times than not, all encompassing I assure you, however, that when our paths do
cross, and our eyes often again, I can say, the pleasure will be mine.

At that time I hope we may share freely our
journey, our plans, our fears and our desires and part
more enlightened and inspired than before.

Sincerely,
Your friend,
Bradley Dittfach

CONTENTS

www.bradleyquick.com

Miracles Happen

I "came to" in May 1987 after suffering years of substance abuse and associated dysfunctional behaviors that led to my being a four-strike convicted felon hanging out on skid row in Los Angeles. It was a spiritual experience that May that put me on the path of self discovery. The story I'd like to convey to you, however, is about one of the many miracles that has happened to me in my recovery. After being involved in emotional, intellectual and spiritual growth for ten or so years, a friend suggested I write a book about my life. The death of my six siblings, the tragic bike accident that left me paralyzed (a bed-ridden vegetable), ending up on skid row, and all my life experiences in between. After a lot of thought and soul searching about having to relive my past, I agreed to write the book.

Throughout my life, I've told others, and convinced myself, that I was many things but an author was never one of them. So I set out to find a ghost writer, someone who would write the book in my writing style, as if I had written it. One day, shortly after beginning this quest, my father called to say he had found a ghost writer who would work with me. I was relieved to say the least. I had a conversation with this woman and she suggested I write five pages about my life. From that she would derive my style, interview me, and write the book. I agreed and thought this a fabulous idea. The next day, there I sat, in front of a dinosaur laptop computer using Word Pad (not knowing any better) to start writing the five pages. When I

www.bradleyquick.com

began pecking away at the keys something very odd happened. I found I couldn't stop, and much to my amazement, ninety days later I had a book! I discovered myself to be an instrument for this message, and though it's based on my experience, I was really not the creator of it. For days, weeks and months, I was inspired. It was all that was on my mind. Whether I was jogging in the morning, sleeping at night, or at work during the day, it was all I could think about, and I spent all my extra time in front of that old laptop computer.

Needless to say, I never called the ghost writer back. I was empowered with the content and ability to write this on my own, and oddly, there are only eight pages about me the book. The majority of the book outlines a process for positive change that is beyond me and what I thought I knew at the time. All of a sudden, I believed I was somebody! I thought of myself as gifted, and one of the chosen few to have this information channeled through me. My ego and delusional pride took off! I thought I was the Second Coming of someone, and much to my surprise, there were those who thought so too. They jumped on the bandwagon, and off we went with my ego and self-delusional pride. These people thought, as I did, that I was a marketable commodity, and my head grew to the point that I could not get thru the door. Any door!

However, every time some *great* promotional endeavor was just about to happen for *me*, *my* new book or *my* process, it would fall through. The bottom always fell out, completely! Continuously discouraged, I always got up, dusted off the humility and went at it again. The same thing happened over and over again finally my fragile ego and pride could no longer put up with the battle. So, two years after the fact, I quit my ego-based self-promotion, got a job and started working for someone else. I gave up my pursuit of superstar grandeur, but persisted with my belief and

www.bradleyquick.com

passion in the cause, and my willingness to be of service to others.

A few months later, while trying to get some normality back in my life, one of the gentlemen I was working with asked if there was any truth to the rumor that I had written a book and, if so, could he read it. I told him I had, and would be honored to give him a copy. He came back a few days later and exclaimed how he had enjoyed the book and thought it could help many people. He then asked if I did any public speaking. I replied, "Of course I do. For me, it's all about carrying the message of self discovery/recovery, change, motivation and life enhancement." He asked if I had anything planned in the near future, and if he could come and hear me speak. I suggested a date and location and he agreed to attend. On that day, we met at the location and went inside. Gathered that night was a crowd of people, most in the group in need of some positive change in their lives. I spoke about my experiences, good and bad, right and wrong, for an hour or so. It went well, and I ended with questions and answers.

When I was done, we went across the street to McDonald's to grab a soda. While sitting there, he looked me straight in the eye, and said, "Bradley, I've made seven international superstars in my day. You're number eight"! Well, a statement like that coming from a friend or an admirer is always kind, but hearing those words from this man almost knocked me off my seat! You see, this fellow was a VP of Motown Record for years, the President of MCA Records, and was responsible for the careers of The Beach Boys, Neil Diamond, Elton John, Barry White, Olivia Newton John and others. He has produced soundtracks for a hundred or more successful movies. To hear those words form him was very flattering, and at once we had a different kind of working relationship.

www.bradleyquick.com

For the next few months, his expert words and advice kept flowing in my direction. At one point he said to me, "Bradley, you need to be on the radio," and he escorted me to KRLA radio in Los Angeles. Before I knew it, I had a one hour weekly radio show that he entitled "The Bradley Quick Experience," based on my self discovery/recovery experience and my book. That was in June 2002.

Since then, on the radio show, I have featured many internationally known celebrities and experts, such as Dr. Wayne Dyer, Melody Beattie, John Bradshaw, Don Miguel Ruiz, and many others. The show went to two hours per week, broadcast live to about four million households, and according to some, it became the fastest growing radio show in Los Angeles. My mentor also suggested I build a website, which I did, at www.bradleyquick.com. All my past radio shows are archived there. We get about 100,000 hits a month, and visitors from all over the US and 62 different countries listen to shows every month. Wow, I'm amazed! The name of the book has changed from "The Bradley Quick Experience" to "The Quick Fix: A Simple Process for Positive Change," and from that book has derived a seminar series entitled "INSIGHT: Purpose, Power, Motivation," currently being conducted in various jails, prisons, institutions, rehabilitation centers, campuses, universities and corporations on a regular basis.

What I am doing now is positively participating in the changing of many people's lives. I believe this has only occurred because I've gotten out of the way of this project's destiny, and my purpose, and have allowed the powers-that-be to guide me by providing me with the opportunities and the willingness to let it happen and not to control it. As long as I was taking credit for all that I had been freely inspired to create, nothing was working. However, the moment my wants, needs, and desires were no longer the focus

www.bradleyquick.com

of my intention and became secondary to the cause of positive change and service to others, miracles began to happen, and continue to happen, again and again. Uncover, discover and discard what you think you know and give in to what can be for you, and watch the miracles happen in your life. Remember, we're in the efforts business not the results business! My hope for you is that you find the miracles in your life and allow them to blossom as I have in mine.

www.bradleyquick.com

INTRODUCTION

All of us at times have really wished we could change our lives in one way or another. Usually, this occurs when we are confronted with situations, and/or feelings and emotions, which we don't wish to or are not equipped to deal with. However, as unfortunate as it may be, we do not change. We just exist and let the wave of negative emotion pass by, then resume our regular activities as if nothing has happened, and again attempt to find our way through life, sometimes blindly and other times with precision.

If your clothes caught fire, what would you do? Maybe run, or try to pat yourself down? Either way, you may very well end up with burnt clothes and first, second or third degree burns all over your body. People educated in burn or fire prevention measures will tell you that if you are confronted with this problem, you should drop, tuck and roll. That in itself will save you from extreme injury and possibly even death. Drop, tuck and roll, to save your life.

If you're on fire you're going to do what the experts have taught you to do to put the fire out, right? At this moment in your life, you may be burning up with substance intake or compulsive behaviors, and don't know how to stop it. You may have tried patting yourself down or running, but this fire just won't stop. It just gets worse for you and rages out of control.

If you can relate to this example, I'd like to share with you how I put out my substance abuse and compulsive behavior fires for good. I'll also share with you the ointments and applications I've used to heal

www.bradleyquick.com

my seemingly badly burned body and my toxic mind. Some call me an expert in the field of substance abuse and behavioral disorder sciences simply because, aside from my education, I have recovered from a hopeless and helpless state of body and mind, one with no future and no possible life. As a direct result of my personal experience, I wrote *The Quick Fix* program to share with others. I discovered a system that really works, if you really want it to and if you're willing to do what it takes. Bottom line, if you will trust this process and study this book, it may very well enhance your life.

If you're anything like me, you want it and you want it now. Immediate gratification has always been my solution. Fix me and fix me now! I'm an immediate gratification junkie at my best. You must realize, however, that this journey may be akin to a slow boat to China. Yet, it may also be the most rewarding voyage you'll ever take, to a place, as yet, you know very little about. Welcome aboard.

I was always ready to surrender my will (what I want), and my life (who I am), to the care of the job, the relationship, the substance(s), to that person, place, thing or situation that fixed me at that moment. But as things went, I always wound up lonely, separate, different and afraid. I was alone again and stuck with myself. This *Quick Fix* process is something you can give your all to, and at the same time be confident that this process will never let you down, never turn its back on you, or leave you hanging. If you work with it, it will work with you. I promise. You didn't get in this situation overnight, so don't expect to get out of it overnight. This process has worked for countless others and it will work for you, if you work with it. It just takes some time, and if you think about it that's all we've got, you and I, is time. So let's make the best use of it!

www.bradleyquick.com

I know that we all think of ourselves as unique or different than others, which in most cases is indeed true and correct. However, those of us engaging in obsessive compulsive behaviors and/or behavioral disorders do have many similarities. And in order for us to achieve our goal of freedom from these behaviors we must explore our similarities more than our differences. You might have begun by sneaking your substance, hiding your behavior, or maybe feeling guilty about participating in certain acts. It could have been fun in the beginning, whether as a child smoking, or drinking at your parents' party, maybe stealing liquor out of the cabinet, taking food to another room or the closet, most likely hiding in fear of getting caught. I would guess that, in time, the behaviors accelerated.

Your abusive behaviors may have come upon you all at once or gradually over time. You have to answer this question for yourself. Deep down inside, you know the answer. We're all different, but all of us began this compulsivity somewhere. And right at this time, right now, you have an opportunity to end it. Despite any differences, this is one opportunity we can all share.

Remember, if you keep doing what you're doing, you can expect the same results! Let's all win, find our purpose, and make the best out of this thing called life.

www.bradleyquick.com

My Life Experience

You may, or may not, relate to my story. Only you can make that determination. However, while reading my life experiences, please keep in mind that if this process can work for me, it will most likely work for you, if you work at it. If you don't, it absolutely won't work for you.

I was born the second eldest in a family of nine — seven children, my mother and my father. By the time I was eight years old, four of my brothers and my only sister had died of cystic fibrosis. The memories I have of that part of my life are not as vivid as one might imagine. Then again, suppressing these memories may be my brain's way of avoiding pain. However, I can only now realize how devastating that time must have been for my parents.

My mother tells me how she and my father would leave the house for the hospital with one of the children, and return without the child in hand, only to find me watching anxiously through the window anticipating their return with my sibling. Upon my acknowledging the obvious, the death of another, I would stand in the corner and say nothing. I could listen to no one's explanation, and show no emotion. I internalized it all; the abandonment, the guilt and the loss.

I started first grade at three years of age, in a private school. They said I was a gifted child. I could speak French and Spanish and was very good in math. My father had even taught me to play chess. Though not apparent on the outside, inside I was reeling from the pain of the loss of my siblings. On a gray November day in 1963, the school made an

NOTE

www.bradleyquick.com

NOTE
---

announcement that President Kennedy had been shot. At that moment, I turned to my teacher, tears running down my face, and told her it was I who had killed the president. I assumed total responsibility and total guilt for this horrific act.

I had an older brother, Bryan, who, because of his sickness, got most of the attention from my parents, grandparents and other family members. So I wanted him out of the picture. When he died, I assumed responsibility for his death, too. I was convinced that it was my fault. I had killed him. The guilt was mine, and I took the guilt of the world upon my small shoulders, even the assassination of the president. As I got ready to start third grade, we moved to a smaller house and I had to change schools, this time attending a public school. My mother met with the principal, who said I was too young for third grade, so at age six they put me back into the first grade. Already familiar with the work, I developed an attitude that "I knew it, why do it?" That attitude would haunt me throughout my life.

Sports became part of my life at about age seven. I played Little League baseball and PeeWee football for the Seaview Sharks. I excelled at both. I played baseball for the Reds. I was their star pitcher and best hitter. They called me Big Bad Brad. I loved sports. I'd always give Coach Cook, my football coach, a hard time. He'd say, "Time for pushups!" My response would be, "What's a pushup?" I guess I thought I was cool, or maybe I was just a smartass. The only problem I had with football is that I hesitated to hit anybody very hard. While athletic, I did not like inflicting pain on others. At age nine, at the beginning of the football season, the second day of fourth grade, I suffered major brain trauma in a bike accident. While walking home from school with the neighbor kids, I had won the opportunity to ride as a passenger with my next door neighbor, on his ten speed bike, down a great big hill. I hopped onto the cross bar and we were off. We soon reached a speed that was estimated to be about 60 mph, hit a bump, and my feet flew into the spokes. It was a bad accident. The doctors said I'd either die by morning or be a bedridden vegetable for the rest of my life.

I underwent a tracheotomy, and was in a coma for a month. It was just about that time that the doctors gave up hope and suggested I be taken off life support. My mother wouldn't have it, and against the doctors' orders, she and my father took me home. Mom slept with me, walked me, talked to me, and pushed me around in a wheel-chair (Thanks, Mom, thanks Dad). I was partially blinded in my right eye. I had no coordination in my left side, and my entire right side was para-lyzed. I could not communicate at all. When I tried, it was usually unrelated to what I was trying to convey. I was a mess. I had to learn to walk and talk all over again, and as if that wasn't enough, I no longer had any coping mechanisms. I had no self-esteem, no self-worth, no self-confidence – all in all, a terrible self-image. Coming out of this, I felt lost. I felt I was no longer enough. I no longer had the ability to deal with life on life's terms, even if just from a child's perspective. The doctors put me on an anticonvulsive drug called Dilantin.

After a couple years of physical, speech and vision therapies, I attempted to integrate back into society's perceived normality. I definitely didn't fit in, and was always striving for attention and accep-tance. At that same time I was struggling with my identity, my parents began a sloppy divorce. My father kidnapped my younger brother, Blair, and me. He took us to Miami, then London. Then, when we arrived back home in San Diego, my mother kidnapped us from him. All this was very unset-tling for a child with no emotional stability. Stare downs with psychiatrists, severe mood swings and

NOTE

www.bradleyquick.com

www.bradleyquick.com

NOTE

a complete defiance of boundaries became a way of life for me. I was a mess.

Blair and I relocated to northern California with our mother and soon-to-be stepfather. I was eleven years old, and I believe it was then that I first found the relief brought forth by substances, including food. I began to smoke cigarettes and drink alcohol, not realizing they diverted me from others, buffered me from life, helped me to fit in and, in fact, may have kept me alive. At least that was what I thought. As my teenage hormones started raging, I found it easy to escape through sex; with self, others or whatever was most handy. I was in trouble all through school. I even got kicked out of a couple, including high school, in the second week of eleventh grade.

I was living with my father at the time, and he said I either had to go to school or get a job. In fact, on several occasions, he took me to his office with him. I never knew exactly why until many years later when he told me that he had hoped he could spark my business interest. I had been oblivious to his intent. The only thing I knew was that I had to find that next fix to feel comfortable, and it didn't matter what, where or who it came from or in what form it presented itself. I smoked cigarettes, drank alcohol, smoked marijuana, stuffed myself with food and tried to have sex with anyone that was willing. It made no difference, and I never worried about the consequences of my behavior. I just didn't want to feel and did whatever was necessary to fix me and fix me fast!

At age nineteen, after being dumped by a couple of women and drinking all day on the hot, sunny beach, a buddy and I decided we needed to get more whiskey and then retire to his place and relax. I used a California ID card I had gotten when I was fourteen. I had been waiting for this chance to use it. When I came out with the whiskey, I saw my buddy arguing with a group of local toughs. Before long an altercation erupted. Shots were fired. We chased them, they chased us. Of course, the cops came and we were arrested. After spending three of the scariest, most brutal days of my life in jail, being bailed out (on four counts of attempted murder), then taking the bus home, I was informed over the phone that my last brother, Blair, had just been killed in an auto accident. Without hesitation, I headed straight for the liquor cabinet. Getting drunk was the only way I knew to deal with the feelings and emotions. I had to call my father in Pennsylvania and relay all this tragic information to him. The first thing out of his mouth was, "Stay out of the liquor cabinet and tell me what happened." I had to tell him how Blair had been thrown out of and rolled over by his buddy's car, how I had been arrested on four counts of attempted murder and that my car had been impounded.

I had always felt lonely, separate, different and afraid, but the intensity and emotion behind my feelings, at that moment, was the worst ever. Up to that point, I had already been addicted to and reliant upon heroin, crystal methadrine, pot, mushrooms, cocaine, reds, cigarettes and alcohol. I'd been in and out of jail, in and out of schools, and a wild sex addict. I loved to indulge in foods of all types, especially during a drug induced case of the munchies. By now, I already had five DUI`s under my belt, and I still wasn't finished.

My father, fully embarrassed by his only living son, soon booted me out of San Diego. I was only allowed to return for court appearances and final sentencing. My father and I knew the judge's best friend and we made that known to the judge. I was convicted on four counts of assault with a deadly weapon and was looking at 4 to 10 years in prison. Due to our indirect affiliation with the judge, I got sentenced to only six months, and ended up doing just 72 days of local time. That was a big relief.

NOTE

www.bradleyquick.com

www.bradleyquick.com

NOTE

The day I got out of jail, I went to a massage parlor, got a car, headed to my connection's house to score some drugs, and by that afternoon was getting drunk, once again, at the beach. My existence was fueled by a need for immediate gratification and I was already dependent upon substance abuse for survival. My father wouldn't tolerate me in San Diego and after wrecking his old Lincoln Town Car, I was soon shipped back to Moscow, Idaho, where my mother lived. There, my overeating, erratic behavior and substance abuse continued to be the focus of my life. By this time, neither of my parents liked me, but just barely tolerated me. They were never sure what I would say or do. I was unpredictable at best, and very scary to be around. As is the case for most alcoholics/addicts, it is seldom the acquaintance or casual friend we hurt or offend. It is always those closest to us, our family and friends. It is always those that meant so much to us, those we truly love, that we drag through the hot coals of embarrassing or humiliating behaviors. It is sad, but very true.

Knowing I had to get out of Mom's house in Moscow, (but not having the money to do so) I resorted to the next best thing; going back to school. As a student at age twenty-two, I could justify continued or even enhanced support from my parents. So I enrolled at Spokane Falls Community College in beautiful Spokane, Washington. There, just as in Moscow, I absolutely did not fit in with my long blonde hair and bellbottoms. I didn't bother to make any real effort to adapt to my surroundings. I felt I had to be different, either better than or less than others. Never an equal, always better or less than.

I had no positive self-identity. I was proficient at the art of lying and self-delusion, and had been that way ever since the bicycle accident. It was never about me; it was about who I knew, or said I knew. It was about who my father was, or who I said he was; the places I'd been, or said I'd been. My ego was based on perceived association, not reality, just my perceived grandiose associations. I really believed all my lies and fabrications. Deep down inside, I felt with all my heart that I was an insignificant, worthless human being. If you would ever see the real me, you would certainly abandon me as I believed my siblings had. You would not pay attention to me, just as my unattainable father paid no attention, and you would certainly not care for me as an individual. You would certainly discard me. I always felt lonely, separate, different, afraid, isolated and alone.

So, back to school I went, false ego and pride in hand, along with my books. I stuck out like a sore thumb, a fish out of water. My father had agreed to finance my schooling, and told me to find an apartment. Rather than feel like I was too much of a financial burden, I found a real dump for a whopping $150 a month. Mom furnished it, and I was set. I got my backpack, found the liquor store, and off to school I went. I hadn't used my brain in a long time. Going back to school was a disaster. While trying to make an impression in my classes and on my classmates, I would ask questions which I thought were absolutely profound, but I only to got laughs and looks of disgust from those around me. As the end of the quarter loomed ahead, I foresaw several failing grades coming up. Having another of my befuddled brainstorms, I dropped out and received an incomplete grade. Better than failing, I thought. Thus continued my first year of higher education.

Suddenly, business law became appealing, my brain began to work a little better, and I got involved in the music industry. That gave me a license to party and instilled some false pride or mistaken importance to my life. Again, I was delighted with myself and constantly made grandiose statements about my supposed importance.

NOTE

www.bradleyquick.com

www.bradleyquick.com

NOTE

"Yeah, I work with *them*, or, "Sure, I'm putting that concert or tour together." My relevance as a human being was entirely based upon what others thought about who I knew or what I did. In my eyes, I was still insignificant and worthless, so any adulation I got couldn't be about me. It had to be about someone or something else with which I claimed to be affiliated. I can only assume that you can either understand or relate to this pathetic state of mind.

One Thanksgiving, after being absent from San Diego or seeing my father for two years, Dad invited me to come and spend the holiday with the family, all 50 or 60 of them. I accepted and talked him into letting me bring my younger half-brother, Bruce, who was only four years old, so that he could meet the Quick family. Up to that point, my father had been hinting that he might, because of my supposed dramatic change, allow me to work with him in one of his businesses. I was thrilled. It was my dream to work with my father and to make him proud. I showed up that Thanksgiving, Bruce in hand, knowing I would be confronted by family, with feelings and emotions running through me that I had no idea how to contend with. Naturally, I resorted to what I did best to cope with every emotion — happiness, sadness, excitement, depression or anger, in hate, in love, or in fear. I again relied on the comfort of substance(s) to deaden my discomfort. At that memorable Thanksgiving reunion I, one more time, made a total ass of myself, embarrassing everyone, sometimes with clothes on, sometimes with clothes off. I awakened the day after with dread, knowing something was wrong but not remembering what it was. I wanted a beer, knowing that would fix my hangover, but I saw the disgust in the eyes of my family members, and knew that was not to be an option. I flew back to Spokane the next day, all hope of working with my father gone. Another opportunity lost to drugs and alcohol.

I was hanging out in bars a lot, some seedier than others. The Fresh Air Tavern was a favorite haunt for me (funny name for a place that always smelled like urine and sickness.) Bill, the owner, and I had something in common. Neither of us could control our use of mind altering substances. We shared completely that knowledge of our powerlessness. One day, while shooting pool, I met a woman named Cindy and immediately invited her to my apartment for dinner. She accepted the invitation, and being as sly and debonair as I thought I was, I made sure I had a bottle of wine and a gram of cocaine. When she showed up, we began to drink and eat. As the evening progressed, I said, "How about a couple of lines, would you like that?" She responded, "Oh yes". I came out of the bedroom, gram of cocaine in hand, and saw her getting something from her purse. "What's that"? I asked. "Oh, this is how I like to do my coke," she said, showing me the syringe in her hand. "Have you ever tried it?" I had previously used needles for heroin, crystal methadrine and, I think, coke on one occasion, but I denied it. She said, "It's pretty good; do you want a blast"? I felt like a god for the duration of that rush. I was God and John Holmes, the well-known porn king, both at the same time.

I continued to feel like that for the remainder of my intravenous drug life. I continued to chase that first "rush," but never again experienced it. It became most apparent to me, during my cocaine use, that I had a hard time doing just one hit. Just one, in fact, of anything. I found it impossible to limit my consumption of anything that made me feel good or brought me instant gratification. I found I couldn't "just say No!" Yes, there was occasionally an exception to my inability to say no or do just one, but those occasions very few and

NOTE

www.bradleyquick.com

www.bradleyquick.com

NOTE

far between and never the rule. My answer was always, "More." I began to write bad checks and go to any lengths to acquire more cocaine and more syringes. I had no idea how I was going to pay my monstrous debt to the cocaine dealer.

Suddenly one day, it dawned on me that I only had two days to drop out of school and still be reimbursed for the out-of-state tuition my father had already paid. Then I could even up with the coke dealer and get more cocaine fronted to me on my good credit. Rescued! What a creative solution to ensure that things would continue to go better with cocaine. If someone told me the definition of insanity was "doing the same thing over and over and anticipating different results," I would not have believed them. But at that point in my life, that definition became my life. In looking back, I believe I was truly insane.

Once again, my substance inflicted behavioral disorders stopped working for me. I was getting evicted, burning all my bridges, dropping out of school one more time, and losing the respect of anyone who, at one time, may have thought well of me. It was time for me, again, to find a geographic solution. I could move and leave all my troubles behind. The truth is, the only problem I had was me. I was my problem. The only troubles I had were of my own creation, my own making. I didn't realize that wherever I went, I took my troubles with me. Soon after that, I ended up in a seedy motel in a bad section of downtown Los Angeles. I had been invited to L.A. by Ed Kim, a friend whom I had known all my life as if he were a brother. He was originally my father's houseboy in the Korean War. He thought he could fix me, mold me into someone respectable. I loved him and appreciated his efforts, but he had no idea of the mental state I was in. My stay at that motel lasted about three weeks, and I was in a continuous drunken stupor. I added visits to sex shops, calls to hookers and endless chain smoking to my behavior, for good measure. Even then, I considered myself in high esteem, grandiose to some extent, while I continued looking for that next fix, that next dose of immediate gratification.

Kim had lobbied my father, to his disfavor, to support me in this "new beginning" in Los Angeles. To my surprise, he did, and I moved to an apartment Ed Kim selected in the middle of Korea town. I was the only Caucasian in the building, let alone the neighborhood. I was the only one that spoke English. Again, I stuck out like a sore thumb, the only non-Asian boy around. Fortunately, I found a local bar three blocks away, perfect stumbling distance. The clientele was predominantly black, but as long as they served me and I got some sense of being socially accepted, it was okay. I fit in. After living in my Korea Town apartment for awhile, I got the lay of the land. I began to hang out in Hollywood at different bars, some seedier than others. I'd talk about the deals I was working on and who I knew and who they knew and what we were going to do. I couldn't stop myself, or slow down, for that would have forced me to see and feel my inner self. I didn't want to feel or see myself. I couldn't have handled it. I was busy running from myself and all my stunted emotions, failings, and amplified sensitivities. My thoughts were moving at a thousand miles per hour. My mind had become my worst enemy.

At one point, for about 10 days in a row, I had no idea how I'd gotten back to my apartment from the various dives I frequented in Hollywood. When I would "come to," I would find the front door of my apartment wide open, oven left on, food all over the place. This scared me. I stopped drinking and drugging at that instant, and was suddenly filled with a burst of enthusiasm for change. I lost 40 pounds in fifty-four days. Nothing compulsive about that! I was running five miles a day in

NOTE

www.bradleyquick.com

www.bradleyquick.com

NOTE

the smog, and swimming three days a week. As always, I demonstrated very compulsive and obsessive behaviors. I've always been that way. Way too much or way too little of everything. I found a job as a private mail courier, taking the bus an hour and a half to and from work each way. Things began to look up, on the outside anyway. Kim talked my dad into buying me a new car and funding yet another move across town. I moved to what I thought was West Los Angeles, on Larrabee Street, right off the Sunset Strip. All the famous clubs —the Rainbow, the Roxy, Gazarries and, of course, the Whiskey a Go Go, were all handy for alcohol, drugs and women. In that West Hollywood period, the only things I was abusing were cigarettes and marble fudge ice cream, eaten by the gallon. My only questionable behavior was excessive masturbation, exercise, and an inability to deal with people on most any level other than saying "hello" and "goodbye."

I had no coping mechanisms, and could not deal with people, places, things or situations as a normal twenty-five year old might. Nor could I get intimate with anyone, at any level, for any purpose, for any amount of time. Talk about nowhere to go! I was bored and extremely frustrated. I was cutting myself off from the world. I became a prisoner in my apartment and between my own ears. Finally, I couldn't handle it any longer. I had to find a way out, but how? Alcohol had made me lose my way home 10 days straight. Ice cream and cigarettes just weren't cutting it any more, and one can only masturbate so many times. What option did I have? Cocaine! That was my answer. I would just shoot coke on the weekends and continue to go to work and exercise. So I became a weekend warrior, partying and spending money. That lasted for about 90 days. The money was gone and I couldn't get to work on Monday mornings. I didn't know what to do. I was hopeless and seemingly helpless yet another time. What does any confused boy do in that situation? Call Mom, right?

That's just what I did, and she sent her new husband with some money to my aid. After a long talk, we went to dinner at Simply Blues, seventeen stories up at Sunset & Vine in Hollywood. It was there he talked me into having a drink. I hesitantly ordered a double Bushmill on the rocks. It came and I began to drink, and all of a sudden, I had a different perception of life and myself. I was able to speak freely and articulately about the world and its inhabitants. I felt better and freer with the opposite sex. My mind began to work. All these miracles in my body and brain, and I hadn't even left the dinner table, let alone set the glass down. I found my answer, alcohol! This was my solution. I was back, but didn't realized that this was the beginning of my end.

In looking back, I've noticed that not only was my mind and body deteriorating with each year, but so were my choices of people, places and things to do. I felt better and maybe even superior hanging around others who had no purpose or ambition in life other than getting loaded. For me, too, it was all about getting loaded. It was, once again, about releasing me from the bondage of self through outside means, whether drugs, sex, alcohol, food, cruising or money. Fix me and fix me now! I now understand that it was *me* that I couldn't stand to be around. I kept myself in that bondage with my issues and my inability to cope with life (people, places, things and situations.)

Two chaotic years later, while in the grips of my substance induced behavioral disorders, I found myself standing on the corner of 6th & Westlake, better known as Skid Row in Los Angeles. I weighed 248 lbs, wore no shirt, and my sweat pants were held up by a piece of rope. A bandage ran up and down my left arm so the needle tracks weren't so obvious. A towel was draped around my neck, and

NOTE

www.bradleyquick.com

www.bradleyquick.com

NOTE

I held the leg of a table in my hand for protection. I had no future, just the hope for another fix, or that death would release me. I was helpless and hopeless. I had a nice apartment and a nice car, both paid for by my parents, yet I was obviously more comfortable standing on that dirty street corner on Skid Row than I was dealing with my life or society and the people in it. It was my best thinking, my best efforts, that had gotten me to that point. Here I was, hanging out, disheveled and loaded on Skid Row and thinking that that was suitable or even acceptable. What problems or situations has your best thinking gotten you into? Think about it, and if your answer does not meet your satisfaction, I've got a solution here that works if you are willing to work it. It's a much better way to go!

After one three or four day run of shooting coke and drinking, I ended up back at my apartment in West Hollywood. I was coming down the backside of my high, a drug induced emotional roller coaster. Impending doom was reaching out to me. Then the phone rang. It was Ed Kim. He asked me how I was doing. I broke down and began to cry, and told him of my current state. Within 45 minutes, he was at my door. Within 24 hours, my mother was there. My mother, bless her heart, came to my aid and took control. Within a few days, she and my father where looking for a hospital to put me in. I did not want to go to a hospital, but I had no choice. I went only to appease them with the thought that I might not lose their love and financial support. On May 11, 1987, my twenty-eighth birthday, they enrolled me into the Substance Abuse Program at Pacific Hospital in Long Beach, California. I considered this a waste of my time and their money. At the hospital, I was locked up with thirty other people, mostly blue collar workers, people using their Workers Compensation and health benefits so as not to lose their jobs.

My fear and humiliation at being there manifested itself as anger; in fact, there was some concern
that, in my rage, I might kill somebody. I thought
the other patients were all losers. I didn't realize
I was just like them, and probably even worse.
The counseling staff showed us videos of people
getting high and loading syringes with drugs. I
began to get dry rushes, just as if I where actually
shooting cocaine. They where also talking all this
nonsense about God, and what did they know? As
a child, I prayed to this thing called God, to save
my brothers and sister, but they died anyway. I had
no concept of God. He certainly hadn't talked to
me lately. Nine days into the program, I continued
to be so disruptive that they were getting ready to
throw me out. My counselor told me I would have
to either leave or hit my knees and try to touch
base with a Power greater than myself.

I thought this was all a bunch of crap; a Power
greater than myself? Not likely. Maybe, I thought,
a judge or the police are greater than me. But a
"higher Power?" I didn't agree with the concept,
but what choice did I have? I had no place to go
except the streets of Long Beach. I was out of good
options. So even though I was uncomfortable,
maybe even scared of doing it, hitting my knees
seemed to be the best option at hand. I got down
on my knees that night and said, "Hey, Bud, help
me out, will Ya? Amen." Then I got up and rolled
into bed. Oddly enough, when I got out of bed
the next day, everything seemed just a little bit
different. My perception was different, the atmo-
sphere didn't seem so bad. My fellow patients, and
even the staff, seemed to be a little different. I got
through that day just a little bit easier. I got on
my knees again that next night and said, "Hey,
Bud, pretty good, keep it up! Amen." I now know it
wasn't what I said, it was the sincerity with which
I said it that made the difference. Although not
a perfect prayer, it was from the heart, a sincere

NOTE

www.bradleyquick.com

_____
NOTE
_____

www.bradleyquick.com

request to the Universe, or whatever, for some help. At that time, death would have been more fun than living in this hopeless and helpless state of body and mind. I got off my knees and got into bed. I awoke the next day and my entire perception of life had changed for the better. Everything started to make sense to me, from what the staff was saying, to what they were having us do. It all made sense, and the only action I had taken was to ask this Thing I did not comprehend, understand or believe in, for some help. What I had was what is known as a profound spiritual experience. My only part in this transformation from death to life was having the willingness to ask for help from Something I neither believed in nor understood.

Don't run away! It's not a religious message that I carry. This is not a religious issue or process. This message is one of C.L.E.A.N. (Clearly Learning Everything Absolutely Necessary) to rid ourselves of this substance induced discomfort, and to have the ability to P.A.C.E. (Positive Action Cures Everything) ourselves with this Quick Fix in hand as our guide to a better life today, tomorrow, and always. A C.L.E.A.N. P.A.C.E. will work for you every time if you work it. This is a positive alternative lifestyle that really works.

I've been on the road to recovery from substance abuse since May 1987. The road has not always been easy. At times, it's been about adversity and pain, both physical and mental challenges, and growth of all different varieties. I just don't give up, and just won't give in to my substance(s), no matter what. No matter what my head tells me, no matter what the circumstances are, no matter what. *Just Right Now!* If we don't give in, we cannot be taken away. I currently speak in hospitals, prisons, corporations and institutions of all types. I carry the message of hope, the message of change and purpose, growth and expansion. I'm not responsible for the abilities I've been so freely given to carry this message. However, I do feel responsible to carry this message, to enhance its content, to broaden its audience, and to remain humble to its purpose. We are looking for similarities, not differences. It's the feelings and emotions, not necessarily the circumstances, that bring us together.

I hope that through this brief glimpse into my experience, you can understand my evolution, and not just compare it to yours, but identify with at least some of it, and see that I have a solution that works. One that works not only for me, but for you as well. I have been in this process successfully since 1987, and I continually find myself growing and changing. I've had to grow up. I've had to mature and become a responsible adult. In doing so, I have joined the human race and now have an opportunity to live life as I was born to this earth to live, to accomplish in this universe what I was put here to do. Whatever my path, wherever that path may lead, my task is to follow it. I shall do my very best, in this moment, to try to set myself aside, get out of my own way, look at the big picture, and see what I can do best for you and those around me. I want to help better your life, so that you, too, may experience an easier glide through this stage of your development.

NOTE

www.bradleyquick.com

CHAPTER 2

Your Body and Mind

www.brianpatrick.com

NOTE

I would like you to understand both the physical and mental effects of abusing substances. Simply put, the substance abuse issue may very well stem from a dysfunction centered in the nervous system. To date, there is no known cure. Today, however, through The Quick Fix process, the problem of substance abuse can be arrested. The medical definition of dysfunction is "a difficult or abnormal function." This is important to understand because it is the basis of why we do many of the things we do. Dysfunction can range from having a headache to having a full-blown disease. Substance abuse is simply an allergy of the body, (your chemistry) coupled with a chemical dysfunction of the mind.

The nervous system controls the body. Substance abuse causes the nervous system to malfunction by creating chemical alterations, or imbalances, within the brain and spinal cord. There are two major parts to the nervous system, the central nervous system (CNS) and the peripheral nervous system (PNS).

The CNS is your brain and spinal chord, the main nerves of the body. The PNS involves automatic functions you don't have to think consciously about, like the beating of your heart. The CNS, together with the PNS, controls every aspect of your physical and psychological being. All of your thoughts, muscle movements, digestion, emotional experiences, senses (taste, touch, smell, sight and hearing), are controlled by your nervous system.

Your heart, liver, kidneys, small and large intestines, lungs, spleen, gall bladder, and adrenal glands are all controlled by the nervous system. These systems, the CNS and PNS, and all other systems in the body, are highly regulated and balanced by the body. The body is consistently balancing three major areas:

1. **Structure** (bones, muscles, joints)
2. **Chemistry** (vitamin & mineral balance, as well as food, alcohol and drugs)
3. **Mind** (emotions)

This is what I call the triad of health. If you have a triangle and one of the sides is dysfunctional, or non-supportive, the triangle will collapse. When the triangle collapses, your body begins to deteriorate. It does not take much for the body to lose its homeostasis (balance). And your body is affected by everything you put into it, from the foods you eat, to the air you breathe.

There is always cause and effect within our bodies. If you abuse your body and your thoughts, with substances and behaviors, your body and mind will retaliate in many ways. Structural, chemical, and/or emotional dysfunctions occur. The bottom line is, if you abuse your body, you will experience, if you haven't already, a collapse of your health. If not corrected, you will have a problem that may not be so easily overcome. There are so many different elements in our world today that may cause dysfunction in our makeup and subsequently lead to substance abuse. There are always negative short-term effects, and certainly negative long-term effects, of substance abuse of any kind.

Following are the realities and effects of some behaviors, substances and chemical imbalances.

Addictive Behavior:

Why is it that not all people develop addictive behaviors? There are many people who may have a drink, do drugs, or eat sweets on a casual

www.bradleyquick.com

www.bradleyquick.com

NOTE
---

basis who do not develop this abusive problem. According to some prominent doctors, there is a fourfold increased risk of developing alcohol and/or drug dependency if you have a close relative that is chemically dependent. The risk factors of developing an addictive personality can relate to a family history of addictive behaviors and/or substance abuse.

Alcohol:

The most commonly abused substance is alcohol. Alcohol is socially acceptable and is not considered a controlled substance. It is so easy to obtain and use that most people don't think they have a problem with alcohol until it's too late. Alcohol attacks the CNS, liver, kidneys, heart and many other body parts. Its primary effect causes sedation and potential hypnosis. In the short-term, alcohol decreases one's inhibitions, increases a false sense of self-confidence, and induces slurred speech and euphoria. These effects can lead to intellectual, emotional and body control impairment. If alcohol is combined with other hypnotic or sedative drugs, your nervous system may very well become depressed and stop functioning.

Continual abuse will affect your liver and cause it to enlarge, develop fatty areas and even cirrhosis (permanent enlargement and damage). A common cause of death is liver cirrhosis and liver failure.

Amphetamines:

These drugs stimulate the central nervous system, thus increasing alertness, decreasing fatigue and causing insomnia. They also can stimulate the release of dopamine, but with less effect. The short-term usage of amphetamines is a heightened sense of alertness, but this can quickly turn into disaster. Long-term effects of these drugs include insomnia, confusion, dizziness, tremors, panic states, psychotic episodes, heart disease with eventual circulation shut down, and anorexia. As your nervous system starts to deteriorate and break down, all of its control over your body starts to deteriorate and break down as well. As you lose mental control, you will also lose physical control and this can ultimately lead to death.

Allergies:

A true allergy within the human body causes a very complex chain reaction that can manifest with a rash, hives, breathing trouble, skin irritation, diarrhea or cravings. Let's focus on cravings. We usually crave things such as sugar, alcohol and drugs because of both mental and physical dependence.

We usually crave things when our body is in a low period of its metabolic cycle, and it is trying to pull itself back into a high point in an effort to normalize and stabilize itself. How many of us feel really tired after eating a large meal, especially a meal of pasta or other high carbohydrate food? One explanation is the sudden drop in blood sugar levels. When the blood sugar drops, we get tired and want to take a nap. Conversely, when we get tired, we usually look for some food that has sugar in it to get "instant energy." Here, your body is trying to normalize its blood sugar level. Alcohol has a similar effect, because alcohol is converted to sugar (and other byproducts) by the body. Therefore, if you have a problem regulating craving's for sugar, this could potentially lead to a craving for alcohol.

Antidepressants - Selective Serotonin Reuptake Inhibitors (SSRI's), MAO Inhibitors & Tricyclics: includes Prozac, Zoloft, Celexa, Paxil, Amitryptylline, Nardil, Luvox

WARNING: IT SHOULD BE NOTED THAT A GRADUAL TAPERING OFF OF MEDICATIONS

NOTE

www.bradleyquick.com

www.bradleyquick.com

NOTE

IS SAFEST WITHDRAWAL METHOD TO AVOID SERIOUS WITHDRAWAL EFFECTS (Often there is the terrible withdrawal associated with the SSRIs. Unless patients are warned to come very slowly off these drugs by shaving minuscule amounts off their pills each day, as opposed to cutting them in half or taking a pill every other day, they can go into terrible withdrawal which is generally delayed several months. This withdrawal includes bouts of overwhelming depression, terrible insomnia and fatigue, and can include life-threatening physical effects, psychosis, or violent outbursts.)

As the most prescribed and abused drugs in America today Antidepressants make the pharmaceutical companies millions of dollars while ruining millions of lives. Keep in mind that these drugs are all serotonergic agents and clones or "copy cat" drugs of Prozac - the first SSRI anti-depressant introduced to the market in America. **Basically what applies to one, applies to the others**. For instance we have more data out on Prozac because it has been around longer, but as the mode of action is the same for all of these meds the effects will be the same for the other drugs on this list as it is for Prozac. If we are discussing one drug, similar effects would be expected from any other company's version of the drug. In fact it **would be more honest to give them the titles of** Prozac #1, Prozac #2, Prozac #3, etc. rather than the brand names they have been given, from the second clone, Zoloft, to the latest Prozac clone, Celexa. My concern is that each new SSRI introduced seems to be a little stronger on serotonin reuptake and therefore potentially more dangerous. And the all too common practice of going from one SSRI to another blocks additional receptors and magnifies the harmful effects of these medications.

It is crucial to learn that according to medical research the theory behind this group of drugs is invalid. Known as serotonin reuptake inhibitors. They are designed to block serotonin in the brain, thereby increasing brain levels of this neurotransmitter. Yet for three decades researchers have been intensely interested in serotonin because LSD and PCP produce their psychedelic effects by mimicking serotonin. **Elevated serotonin is found in: psychosis or schizophrenia, mood** disorders, organic brain disease, mental retardation, autism and Alzheimer's. While low levels of the metabolism of serotonin (which also produces high serotonin), are found in those with: depression, anxiety, suicide, **violence, arson, substance abuse**, insomnia, violent nightmares, impulsive behavior, reckless driving, exhibitionism, hostility, argumentative behavior, etc. The drugs increase serotonin and decrease the metabolism of serotonin leading to any and all of the above results. **This information is extremely crucial for patients** and physicians to learn as soon as possible. We have a high rate of use of these drugs nationwide. Raising serotonin and lowering the metabolism of serotonin in such a large number of people can produce very serious, widespread and long term problems for all of society.

Cocaine:

Increases the brain's ability to release a hormone called dopamine. Dopamine is the body's natural pain medication, and its release into our system can give us a sense of euphoria. However, cocaine quickly starts to deplete the body's ability to produce dopamine, and one then becomes dependent on the drug to produce good feelings.

This drug is commonly known as the "feel good" or "pick me up" drug. Cocaine can also mimic the sensation of having an adrenaline rush, because of its stimulatory effects. The short-term effects of cocaine are increased motor activity that can lead to tremors and convulsions. The long-term effects are strokes, severe depression,

NOTE

www.bradleyquick.com

www.bradleyquick.com

NOTE
---

anxiety reactions, increased blood pressure, heart attacks, sweating, and paranoia. Severe physical depression is seen frequently. Perforation (a hole) in the nasal septum, many transmitted diseases, including AIDS from dirty needles, and complete dysfunction of the respiratory system, are all added dangers of cocaine usage. Again, long-term use of cocaine can kill.

Diabetes:

Adult onset diabetes is epidemic today. Many children are also receiving this diagnosis. This problem, in most cases, is caused by the body's inability to handle excess sugar. By that time, the body is just worn out and can't handle any more sugar. The average American consumes 150 pounds of refined white sugar every year. A diet of high sugar causes dysfunction in the body's ability to handle the excess sugar, and it just gives up. In this case, the intake of sugar has been in such high quantity for such a long period that that the liver, pancreas and adrenal glands can't produce enough hormones to help sugar get processed into the cells. This is where the concept of an allergy comes into play.

Downers or Central Nervous System (CNS) Depressants: includes Barbiturates, such as Mebaral and Nembutal, and Benzodiazepines, such as Valium, Librium, and Xanax.

These drugs are sometimes referred to as sedatives, Reds, or tranquilizers and are commonly taken for anxiety. Valium is one of the most commonly used and abused sedatives today. These drugs are often prescribed for anxiety, schizophrenia, and for people who have spasticity as seen in Multiple Sclerosis and Cerebral Palsy. For most, though, the short-term effects of hypnotic drugs like these are drowsiness, impaired walking, and loss of coordination. The long-term effects are hallucinations, chest pain, severe depression, loss of long-term memory and death.

Barbiturates are another kind of drug that produce similar effects as hypnotic drugs. These sedatives are usually used to help people that suffer from seizures, anxiety and nervous tension. However, barbiturates have been the leading cause of death among suicides for many decades. The overdose of these drugs causes poisoning in the brain, muscles and even fat tissue. They will produce hypnosis (artificially produced sleep), followed by anesthesia (loss of feeling and sensation), and finally a coma and death.

Food:

One abused substance that is gaining more attention today is food, and the fact that many people suffer from overeating or starvation (anorexia). All of your body's normal functions rely upon what you put into your body as fuel. "Your chemistry" is vital in maintaining proper health and homeostasis. In today's society, many of the foods we eat have lost their maximum nutritional value and most foods consumed today are eaten on a convenience basis. Most people find that fast foods, processed foods, frozen dinners and "snack" foods are easier to buy and eat than going home to prepare broccoli, lean protein (fish, chicken, or turkey) and a salad. Having that next bowl of peanuts with a cocktail is a full meal for some people, and this does have a direct effect on the body.

If you pay attention to the ingredients in most convenience foods, you will see partially dehydrogenated oil. Eat this stuff with caution. This oil is used to cheapen the cost of production and increase the shelf life of the product. This chemical will cause your liver to get very angry. It takes approximately 47 days for your liver to filter out partially dehydrogenated oil from your body. This means

www.bradleyquick.com

www.bradleyquick.com

NOTE
---

that your body has to work extremely hard because of a food you decided to put into your mouth. This increase in stress to the liver will cause deficiencies in other areas of liver function. The liver may not be able to maintain your blood sugar level, or may not be able to filter your blood to remove other harmful substances. There is always cause and effect within our bodies.

If we eat too many spicy foods, we could get an upset stomach. If we eat greasy foods, and our bodies cannot tolerate them, we could get diarrhea, break out, and/or get sluggish. If you abuse your body, it will retaliate in many ways. "Your chemistry" is a delicate balance of nutrients that affects your core functions. Your hormones, enzymes, blood, bones, muscles, etc., are so dependent on what you eat, that any excess or deficiency will lead to the body's inability to function properly. If you eat too much of a specific food, then the rest of your dietary needs lack. If everyday, you get that double cheeseburger, fries and soda, you are feeding your body lots of fats and carbohydrates, and what you are not feeding your body is important vitamins essential for proper body function and mental health.

LSD:

Lysergic Acid Diethylamide, LSD, or Acid are names of this same drug that is classified as hallucinogenic. An additional hallucinogenic drug that is commonly used is Phencyclidine or PCP. LSD and PCP attack the brain and start to effect the mood centers and the visual areas of the brain. LSD hits the mechanisms within the body that can change how your heart beats, how your blood pressure can rise, and breathing can get out of control. In addition, the brain will send you through hallucinations that may consist of brilliant colors and anything else the mind can conceive. You get that "psychedelic" feeling that can become a panic attack ("bad trip"). The long-term effects can produce permanent psychotic changes in perception.

Marijuana:

Pot, weed, grass, chronic, herb are just some of the names used to describe the psychoactive constituents present in crude extracts from the hemp plant. It includes the compound tetrahydrocannabinol (THC), cannabidiol (CBD), and cannabinol (CBN). Pot can cause a feeling of euphoria, decreased inhibition, uncontrollable laughter and changes in perception. It can also cause paranoia. Mental concentration is difficult, and you become slothful. Long-term effects include weight gain, impaired judgment and reflexes, as well as depression. However, the specific hazards of using pot are unknown at this time, but there is evidence of lung cancer that has been associated with smoking.

Nicotine:

There are literally thousands of chemicals in one cigarette that have a toxic effect on the body. One of the main addictive substances found in cigarettes is the narcotic nicotine. Nicotine is second only to alcohol as the most abused drug, and is tougher to kick than heroin. Nicotine grabs hold of a person because of its highly addictive properties. It initially produces arousal and relaxation with some degree of euphoria, but leads to serious problems. Nicotine also causes an initial stimulation of the CNS (central nervous system), where it increases your blood pressure, your breathing rate, your intestinal movement and your heart rate. Nicotine affects the part of the brain that participates in controlling your sense of taste, your ability to breath effectively, your ability to hold your head up, and your body's ability to regulate blood pressure. It also dries out skin, and a longtime smoker can often be identified by extremely wrinkled skin, especially on the face. Long-term effects of

www.bradleyquick.com

www.bradleyquick.com

NOTE

smoking can also include, intestinal cramps, lung cancer or cancer to any other part of the body, birth defects, loss of taste, paralysis of your respiratory center, heart disease and death. Don't think for a minute that it's not killing you.

Opiates or Opioids - Pain Relievers: Oxy-Contin, Codeine, Percodan, Fentanyl, Vicodin (Hydrocodone), Morphine, Percocet, Demoral.

These drugs are used to treat a wide range of problems that range from nausea to emotional disorders. Opiates attack your brainstem, where they can mediate your breathing, coughing reflex, blood pressure regulation, nausea and vomiting. Opiates also attack your medial thalamus and disrupt pain that is frequently emotionally influenced. These chemicals have an affect on your spinal chord by making your joint receptors dysfunction, causing the muscles to dysfunction as well. They also affect your hypothalamus (a structure in your brain that controls hormone secretion), and your limbic system (the emotional center in the brain). Morphine's short-term effects can lead to vomiting, increased pressure in the brain and spinal chord, decreased sexual arousal, blurred vision and euphoria. Long-term effects of morphine produce respiratory depression, low blood volume circulated throughout the body, fluid accumulation around the lungs and even lung failure. Heroin has many of the same effects as morphine. The biggest difference between the two is that heroin crosses into your brain more rapidly than morphine and leads to a more exaggerated euphoria. It is easy to overdose on these drugs and death may very will ensue.

PCP:

PCP can produce hallucinations, too, but it has its own set of dysfunctional capabilities. The short term effects of PCP actually block the release of dopamine. As stated earlier, dopamine is a natural chemical in the body and is the very substance that the body secretes to the brain to produce your "high". The brain responds to PCP by shutting down its own dopamine release mechanisms, and you become dependent on the drug to get a "high" feeling. In addition, PCP has anesthetic qualities, and can produce insensitivity to pain, as well as causing severe hallucinations. This drug can also lead to numbness in your arms and legs, an unstable walk, and muscle rigidity. Long-term use can send you into a coma and then lead to death.

The results of using these drugs may vary but it is also likely that while under the influence of hallucinogens such as these, your aggressive tendencies will dramatically increase, and you may inflict pain and/or hazard upon yourself and others.

Self-Sabotage:

This can be defined as the unintentional defeating of your own best interests, making decisions detrimental to your own well-being, then wondering why you have limited your own progression. It often goes hand in glove with sssociating with the same people over and over again who abuse substances, or going to the same places where substance abuse and behavioral disorders are prevalent. These are the very places where you now, or at one time, felt some association, even though detrimental to your self-image and well-being. You might as well be doing drugs everyday! It's generally pretty hard to overcome self-sabotage, because even though your intent and purpose are pure, your core beliefs and subconscious programming are suspect and the real block between you and your intended desire.

NOTE

www.bradleyquick.com

www.bradleyquick.com

NOTE

Examples: Doing the same thing over and over again, anticipating different results. Saying one thing and doing another. Stumbling over your own feet and getting in your own way. Taking inappropriate actions and/or saying inappropriate things.

The key to overcoming any prolonged dysfunctional behavior, self-sabotage spurred by core beliefs, is to consistently engage in positive action (take the body, the mind will follow), and to change the inner "self talk" by reprogramming your inner motives and your true core beliefs. You can do this by using the unique learning process I call *Positive Chat Power*, the F.A.S.T. C.L.E.A.N. P.A.C.E. for positive change.

It is important to know that some of the negative biochemical changes that have taken place in your body can change for the better very quickly, and some can take a lifetime to change. Your body's emotional memory is very powerful and you may have to relearn how to deal with society on society's terms. You may have to learn how to work again, how to regain healthy, non-destructive social skills, and how to deal with life on life's terms. The message is that overtime you can do all of these things and that none of this has to be done by yourself. That is one of the main differences here. Even though you may have addictive behavior, you can still recover. Your body and mind have the ability, with the proper course of action, to heal and correct themselves; it just takes time and effort. The Quick Fix process is always here for you. Take charge of your body and your life.

References by: Dr. John G. Sherman,
Beverly Hills, California.
and
Dr. Ann Blake Tracy - Author
Prozac: Panacea or Pandora?

CHAPTER 3

It's Only a Mistake
If You Don't Learn From It

First, I want you to understand that I know none of this is your fault. Your body and/or mind's inability to deal with your substance(s) or disorders in a rational manner is not your fault. It just so happens to be the hand that you were dealt, not the one that you selected nor the one you deserve. I understand that and believe it to be true, I really do.

Then again, from this point on, you must assume responsibility for your behavior, because now you understand the problem *and* the solution. You now know there is a way out. You know that you no longer have to treat yourself and others in this abusive fashion. You must take personal responsibility for your current state, and quit blaming others for it. For me, it was always someone else's fault, never my own. I was always the victim, pointing my finger at everyone else. I was quick to see the faults of the world and those in it, but slow to ever admit to any fault of my own.

Once, while driving my first car, I pulled out of a parking lot and rear-ended the car in front of me. I reported this to my father as not being my fault, but the fault of the other driver which, of course, I believed it to be. He replied, "Why do you think they call it an accident?" He meant that it was not intentional, nobody meant to do it, but I must assume responsibility for it. After all, I was a part of it.

Let's you and I assume the responsibility for working this process, for that alone is going to take immense faith and courage on your part. Just have faith in this process, and the positive outcome of

www.bradleyquick.com

31

www.bradleyquick.com

NOTE
---

working this process. This faith must be accompanied by trust in the moment and trust in the outcome, followed by an absolute acceptance of your situation. You are what you are, here and now, with infinite possibilities on the horizon, but you are what you are right now, in this moment. That you must accept. You must carry the idea that being of service, even if just minimally, will benefit you. Think about it! If you can get out of yourself by being of service, in any way, to someone else, even if just for a moment, it will benefit you. And you must have the complete realization that this time, this place, this situation, this urge will pass. It will eventually be no more. It always will pass. Let's not forget this. *Faith, Acceptance, Service, and This Too Shall Pass. (F.A.S.T.)* This is what has worked for me, and this is what will work for you.

I'm sure you are familiar with the phrase "cause and effect". Up to this point, most of us, along with our substance(s) and behavioral disorders, have been the very root, or cause, of our situation. Something happens when we use and abuse and/or act out, (cause) and we end up suffering the result (effect) of such action. This is pretty basic stuff. Change the undesired cause, and you may very well end up with a desirable result, or effect. This reminds me of something John Lennon once wrote: "Instant Karma's gonna get you, gonna hit you right in the head, better get yourself together darling, or pretty soon you're gonna be dead." So when you combine distorted "cause and effect" with self-pity, self- sabotage, or lack of self-esteem and self-worth, you end up with undesirable circumstances. Chaos between your ears, to say the least. Let's begin to fix it today, okay? Good cause, good effect. Bad cause, bad effect. Remember: Positive Action Cures Everything (P.A.C.E.).

One problem is that usually our perception is distorted (typically amplified), which affects the "cause". Therefore, our response, or "effect", to a particular "cause" is too distorted to form a positive or appropriate response, usually sadness, over excitement, depression, or anger. Most often our reaction is one of abundance, overreaction. Example: The "fight or flight" syndrome. We start swinging or start running, just like our primitive ancestors did. Or we dull the syndrome through substance abuse or participation in our favorite disorders, or whatever is available at the time. That's about as far as any of us ever get. Fix, fight, or run!

Let's now look at the big picture, the entire show. Imagine you can see from beginning to end, the start and finish of everything. You might desire to yell out to those you love, "Stop, you really don't want to do that!" or, "No, not left, go right!" Whatever is needed so those you love do what you think is best for them.

Since we don't have a crystal ball, we can't always immediately see the positive or negative results of our efforts. We therefore must rely on doing our very best in this moment, and every moment, one moment at a time. This ideal, combined with our willingness to rely upon the experience of those that have gone before us, allows us to stay in the game, and do what needs to be done right now. What a relief, the realization that this production (life), will get along much better if I just stick to playing my part, reading my lines, and only my lines, one word at a time, instead of trying to run the whole show. Focus on your part, on your role, and leave the results to the evolution of the process. You, who often cannot even control yourself, should hardly attempt to control the universe!

Remember, you are in the efforts business, not the results business. Your focus, from this point on, with this process in mind, is to suit up, show up, put one foot in front of the other, do the job that's put in front of you to the best of your ability, and

NOTE

www.bradleyquick.com

33

www.bradleyquick.com

NOTE

stay out of the results. You have control over your efforts most all the time, and you only have expectations in regards to the outcome, or the results, most all the time. On the other hand, I'm sure there are some who are analytical to the extreme. If this is the way your mind works through problems, you might still be thinking how you should, or how you could, have better responded to a given situation. Or you're curious, as smart as you are, as to why you're unable to think yourself into different circumstances. I'll save you a lot of time. It's much easier to act yourself into positive thinking than it is to think yourself into positive action. P. A.C.E. Don't ponder this too long, for it is true. Just accept it and move on.

Don't hang out in places where substances are being used or where the people are who participate in such behavior, and you'll have a much better chance of living without it. It's true! The less you surround yourself with what or who ails you, the more inclined you will be not to participate or indulge in it. If you can just reach out and grab it, if it's just right there in front of you, and that sudden uncontrollable urge, (you know the one) is upon you, you're in big trouble. You lose again, so stay away from it.

About some of those people we admire, (you know, those that claim to be our friends, our "using buddies"): they may appear to be happy when hearing of our change, but they will always continue to try, even if unintentionally, to bring us back to that familiar abusive state. They will say things like, "Oh, just one more," or, "You've been doing so well, you can handle it," or, "C`mon, one won't hurt," or "Hey, don't be so weak," or the ever popular, "Just one for old times sake." The list of things they will say is endless, and they will say them, all in an attempt to pull us back to that place from which we came, that place that we no longer desire to be, that place of familiarity to them.

On the other hand, sometime in the future, these same individuals, after witnessing your positive change, may come to you seeking help and advice as to how to rid themselves of their seemingly hopeless state of body and mind. At that time, if you stick with this process, you will have the answer. Mad, glad, sad, good or bad, we must rely on, and have faith in, this process. It's your choice! Which would you rather be in, fear or faith? It's one or the other.

Let's recap what has been covered thus far.

1. Commonality. Most of us, whatever our background and circumstances, share the same mindset within a few variations. Before you say, "Not me," remember we're looking for the similarities, not the differences. The truth is that all of us desire to be free from substance abuse and behavioral disorders. Happy, sad, excited, depressed, or angry, we drank, used, and/or abused our "fix(s)." That we have in common. Allow the Quick Fix to be your guide to freedom from substance abuse and/or behavioral disorders. This works! It really does.

2. Perception. "Feelings", the way that we perceive the world around us, are often quite different than how the world, people, and circumstances really are. We have a distorted interpretation of reality. Our beliefs, thoughts, base instincts, ideas and mind, plus many of the things we learned while trying to grow up, just may not be true. They are often fear or shame-based with a self-preservation motive. To some extent, our filter is broken. The truth is that we are perceiving life today through the lens of our past experiences.

3. Reaction. "Emotions", how we interpret and respond to people, places, things and situations, can set the tone for our lives. If you think about it, up to this point anyway, there are a lot of

www.bradleyquick.com

www.bradleyquick.com

NOTE

responses or reactions you would have, or should have, done differently, right? "If only I hadn't!" "I said what?" "I really didn't do that, did I?" "No, not me"! Does this sound familiar? It's all about your reaction or response to outside stimuli and the world. Let me ask you a question. If you are not properly interpreting the messages you receive, how can you offer a true and proper response? That's right, you can't! You've got the answer, and right now it's in your hands!

4. Feelings are Facts, they are *not* Truths. The fact is, you feel the way you feel even though that may be far from the truth of the situation. It might not be what's really happening. Our feelings are very easily distorted by our altered perceptions, influenced by anger, fear, lack of food sleep, etc. We are animals of extreme hypersensitivity.

5. Change. Everything that didn't work for you yesterday will most likely still not work for you today or tomorrow. If you keep doing what you're doing, you'll keep getting what you're getting. If you want something different, you have to do something different. No change!, no gain! P.A.C.E. Positive Action Cures Everything!

6. Coping Mechanisms. The ability to cope with feelings and emotions requires putting certain mechanisms to work. Typically, our natural coping mechanisms have been stunted due to our continued substance abuse, obsessions, disorders, etc. In chronological years, we are of one age. In our ability to cope with life on life's terms, we are generally a lot younger. How young you are is simply gauged by the age that you began to rely upon substances, instead of your natural abilities, to cope with situations, feelings and emotions. Some of us began relying on something from the outside to fix our insides a lot earlier in life than others. For that reason, relying upon outside stimuli to help us cope, our emotional growth stopped earlier. As the direct result of that, some of us recover from the effects of substance abuse and behavioral disorders more rapidly than others. Give yourself a break, and remember: you're a winner, so easy does it!

7. F.A.S.T. Faith in this process. **Acceptance** of ourselves, people, places, things, situations. **Service** to ourselves and others. **This too shall pass,** it always does and it always will.

You first must let go, trust, and have faith in this process. If you do, it will work for you. I promise it will. It's better than being rebellious and continuing to do just the opposite, sabotaging your efforts and your future. You've tried other means. Where have they gotten you?

- **Self-reliance,** also selfishness or self-centeredness. Relying on yourself and your skewed thinking got you into this mess. Allow this process to aid you in your thinking.
- **Expectation** of self and others. This is a recipe for disappointment and frustration. Keep an open mind.
- **Self-pity** *I, I, I, me, me, me, my, my, my. Poor me, poor me,* pour me further into my obsessions, disorders, substance(s), etc. You again lose don't you?
- **Stuck in the Problem** with an unwillingness to look at the solution. It's another way of giving up.

It's your choice. I hope that you'll choose the easier, softer way. This is a positive, alternative lifestyle method designed to help you get out of that hell between your ears. You deserve to be set free. Stop messing around. This is for you.

Let me now share something with you that has been a real lifesaver for me over my many years of freedom from substance abuse. I learned, three years into discovery of the meaning of C.L.E.A.N. (Clearly Learning Everything Absolutely Necessary),

NOTE

www.bradleyquick.com

www.bradleyquick.com

NOTE

that the amount of time that I must stay substance and disorder free, (free from that first drink, puff, pill, bite, act, or whatever), is not today, not an hour, but *Just Right Now!* One day, my car took me and a pocket full of money to where I used to score dope and syringes. My head said that I was going there for one reason, but I soon realized I was going there to get loaded. Upon that realization, at that very moment, I threw my commitment to remaining substance abuse free one day at a time right out the window, and instead realized that if I stay substance abuse free just in this moment, just right now, I'll be OK. What a relief! And to acknowledge this realization, all I did was snap my fingers and say to myself, *"Just Right Now!"* Sometimes I must just keep snapping my fingers, as I did then, until the urge passes. And it does; it *always* pass. Think about it. We've just reduced the time involved in avoiding substances and disorders to the ridiculously easy, haven't we? We've reduced the amount of time that you don't have to use or abuse to *Just Right Now!* Snap your fingers and say, *"Just Right Now!"* It really works. Stay in the moment. After all, yesterday is gone and tomorrow may never come, so all we have is just this moment, today. Snap your fingers and say, *"Just Right Now!"*

Another method of reinforcement against using and abusing, and "stinking thinking," is to just shake your head "No!" Before you could even talk, you were communicating your unwillingness to accept things into your little world, by shaking your head from side to side, indicating, "No, I don't want that." You can have the same reinforcement today, anytime, day or night, just by shaking your head "No!" Whenever the thought of indulging in a substance or undesired behavior comes into my mind (and I still do have those thoughts from time to time), I now automatically shake my head "No." It has for me become an automatic conditioned response. Shake your head "No," reinforcing your determination not to submit to something that will only prolong your agony and bring you bad results.

Remember, for us, one drink or one drug is too many, and a thousand never enough. So long as we don't take that first one, we'll be all right, no matter what our head says. Now, if we take away the substance(s) and behaviors that have become our solution for so long, what does that leave us? Yes, ourselves and our life, living without our perceived solution for coping and dealing with life on life's terms. Our inability to deal with life is one of the big reasons why we abused anyway. Remember that never ending cycle? We used substances and behaviors to live, and lived to ingest substances and act out inappropriate behaviors. A certain death sentence. Again we must find faith, a positive solution. We must find something other than our harmful disorders to rely upon, and that must be followed by a willingness from within to do whatever it takes to maintain faith in this process, faith that this will work for you. You can achieve freedom from your substance abuse and disorders. You alone can't, but together we can, so let's do it! There is an answer here that sure beats sitting around feeling sorry for yourself with no hope or solution.

H.O.W.—Honesty, Open-mindedness and Willingness.

These three attributes, combined with what has been written thus far, is your key to being the individual you have always wanted to be. They are your key to learning how to live life without using and abusing. Remember, it's not easy growing up, but it's well worth it!

NOTE

_____

www.bradleyquick.com

www.bradleyquick.com

NOTE

P.A.C.E. yourself! Positive Action Cures Everything, it really does!

We have come to believe that self, manifested in various ways, is the root of most all our troubles today. Preoccupation with self runs the gamut — self-preservation, self-pity, and self sabotage. We are capable of exhibiting all three, sometimes in unison. Given those attitudes, we usually possess a very critical judgmental nature, one of verbal attack and condemnation, sometimes without investigation. We sit in our recliner and attack and criticize others as if we have the upper hand and know everything. Then again, we may be completely manipulated by our surroundings and subject to all the people around us, seemingly without a voice, while holding grudges against most. Neither of these are satisfactory for a happy and joyous existence.

Let's, just for a moment, put ourselves in the other guy's shoes. Yes, I'm referring to that individual that just cut you off, stole your parking spot, or even that person that just doesn't look like you think he should or act like you think he should act. Imagine for a moment you are him, because at some time in your life you have been him in someone else's eyes. It's OK when you do it, but it's certainly not OK when it's done to you. Judgment of others and their actions is not good for me, nor is it in my best interest. It brings with it anger, fear, grandiosity, rage, frustration, and/or envy. To judge someone is to judge ourselves. To judge ourselves is to assume that we are better than or not as good as we should be. In fact, we are neither better nor worse, we are just as we are at this moment. And we are all the same, in many ways. After all, those that we look at and associate with, they're just other human beings doing this thing called life the best way they know how. They too are full of fears, anxieties, ego and expectations of how they think life should be at any given moment. They have their own perceptions. Most of the time, the actions of those we perceive as getting in our way are taken not to impede us but to enhance what they perceive to be their course at that time.

We all have been stuck in rush hour traffic, frustrated to the hilt, full of anxiety and expectation because the traffic is not moving to our desire, only to slam the steering wheel while thinking aloud, "Don't they know I have to be somewhere, don't they know I'm in a hurry? Hey, buddy, get out of my way!" We've all been there, haven't we? It's at that moment, that moment of total self-obsession, that we fail to realize we are not the only ones caught in this traffic jam, we are not the only ones with some place to go, or some place to be, we are not the only ones with an agenda being altered by our present circumstance. The question is, are we just sitting calmly, taking it as it comes, or are we getting overly agitated about that over which we have no control? I believe the latter to be true. It's not often I can admit powerlessness over my current situation.

However, that traffic jam that I have no control over is much like my life, the people, the places, and situations that I come across in my life and that are put in my path. I am powerless and have no real control over what or who is put in my path of life. However, I do have all the power and control in the world over how I accept, respond, and react to that which I am dealt in life.

None of us, you included, are going to be willing to do what it takes, to achieve the desired result, of no longer being dependent on using and abusing, until we finally reach that crossroad of life or strife. The crossroad between being functional and nonfunctional, being appropriate or inappropriate, acceptable or unacceptable. If you think you have reached that point, ask yourself, "Am I done digging?" The moment you stop digging, you'll hit the bottom, and most of us must hit bottom before

NOTE

www.bradleyquick.com

NOTE

www.bradleyquick.com

we'll accept a friendly hand to help us up and out of this pit of misery. You make up your mind, this is your decision, and you'll have to live with the positive or negative outcome of this choice. I will tell you, however, that once you've made the decision for positive change, your life will never be the same. You may even find yourself suddenly full of enthusiasm and vigor for life, excited about being with and helping others, and ready to be all that you can be. This is my experience, and it can be yours.

Even though you have now awakened to the idea, and had the realization that your life can and will get better (and then even better using this process), don't think for a minute that those once fond memories of pleasure and comfort associated with your favorite substance(s) or behaviors will not return. At times, they will be even more vivid and inviting than ever. You will, at times, have absolutely no recall of that detrimental state that led you to that place of total despair, that place of seemingly no return. It's for that very reason we cannot for an instant forget from where we came. If we do, it's only a matter of time before we return to that state of pitiful and incomprehensible demoralization. It has been suggested that maybe we should put on paper a dozen or so of our most reckless substance induced escapades, the ones we're not at all proud of, so that at these times of sudden remembrance we may take a moment and reflect as to where behavior like that being contemplated has taken us in the past. Remember, one is too many, and a thousand not enough, ever. You can do this one moment at a time. *(Just Right Now)* If you will put the same effort into this process as you put into using and abusing, you should have no problem. In fact, if you maintain this method consistently over a reasonable amount of time, it will eventually become a working part of your mind. A new way of thinking, a new attitude and outlook upon life will emerge. In fact, the more you apply these methods to your daily life, the more positive outcomes you will experience and, the more positive the experiences, the more willing you are to continue this process. What a relief, a positive second chance.

Let's cut the niceties. You've got three choices.

1. You can commit suicide. We've all thought about it. You can do it. I wouldn't suggest it, but you could kill yourself. However, if you do, you'll be killing the wrong person. Think about it, at that given moment you're only wanting to kill your feelings and emotions, not truly eliminate your existence.
2. You can continue your substance abuse and stay in your self-manufactured misery. It is made by yourself and it is miserable. But remember, you built the ship you're on, you made the bed you're in and now you must sleep in it.
3. You can trust and have faith in this process, study this handbook, and begin to live in the solution for positive change, so that you may help yourself and others to and through a better life experience.

The choice is yours, 1, 2, or 3, and it doesn't take a rocket scientist to figure out which one holds the best future for you and your loved ones. This is all about picking up where you left off some time ago, before the trouble, before the mental turmoil, before the separation of family and/or friends. How many times have you heard, "You've got such potential. Why don't you do something with yourself besides cause problems?" We've all heard that, some of us more than others, but we've

NOTE

www.bradleyquick.com

www.bradleyquick.com

_____ NOTE _____

all heard it and many other comments as bad or worse. Again, the choice is yours and only yours. This time, make the right decision, make the positive choice.

CHAPTER 4

WHY ME? (A Good Question)

The answer to this question will vary depending on who you ask, what school of thought they're from, and what their first hand experience is. Some will say it's an allergy of the body, an obsession of the mind, coupled with a spiritual malady, like a disease (dis-ease). Some will say it is an obsessive compulsive disorder, meaning you want it, and you want it now. Then you usually want more. And you always have a hard time stopping, if you can stop at all before passing out, or burning out.

Some will say it's chemical dependency, others will say we're losers, making the wrong decisions voluntarily, and still others will say that we're not concerned about the well-being of those affected around us. (Au contraire, Oh wise one!) Others might even say it's the work of the devil, the fault of another, or that you're just the product of your environment. Then again, if you don't have a ticket, or you're not already, for this harsh merry-go-round called substance abuse and behavioral disorders, maybe you can "Just Say No." But if you're already on this abusive ride, "no" is a virtual impossibility.

There is, most assuredly, a bit of truth in all of these opinions. I'm not disputing them, but I'm sure you'll agree that whatever opinion a particular individual holds, it is their truth. The fact is that using and abusing is now a real issue in our lives. We didn't plan it this way. You most certainly have become the individual that you didn't necessarily want to become. This is just the way it is right now, today. Don't worry; (Yes, the cat's out of the bag) all those people around us, especially those

www.bradleyquick.com

www.bradleyquick.com

NOTE

we're closest to, usually know all about our using and abusing issues. It's much like that elephant nobody has admitted is standing in the middle of the room. Out of fear, nothing is said, and the hope is maybe it will just go away. But it never does. It only gets bigger and more intrusive in all aspects of our lives.

Here's the way I see it. It all started for us when we found the pleasure and/or relief provided to us from the substance(s) or behaviors in question. For a long time, using and abusing substances and/or behaviors was the solution to our problems, they brought us comfort. That pleasure, comfort or relief provided by these destructive actions, substances and behaviors may have been generated by different desires such as fitting in, escape, avoidance (more about this later), subconscious self-sabotage, the physical sensation and many more. Whatever the reason(s), it has led to our current state of affairs; constant or consistent self-abuse and discomfort and inner turmoil. Maybe your affliction is only periodic, yet still troublesome and worth eliminating. After we found that immediate relief or immediate gratification could be achieved through using and abusing, it was much easier to take the substance route than to rely on our own coping abilities, or lack thereof, to manage the situation. After all, which do you prefer, pain or pleasure? For me, my instincts tell me that pleasure should win out every time. Thus, affliction and dependence is born. My intuition, however, let's me know that mere pleasure is not always the best choice.

The issue is, once you've started using and abusing on a consecutive basis, your natural coping mechanisms, the ability to deal with feelings and emotions, ceases to mature. Its natural progression stops. Think about it. Happy, sad, excited, depressed or angry, in fear or in love, we again resort to our disorders. This continued substance abuse response to our perceived situations has created a vicious cycle where, in order to deal with our feelings and emotions, we must submerge them in our substance(s) or behaviors, then be a recipient of the consequences. We must use and abuse our substance(s) or disorders in order to deal with life as it presents itself. It's becomes a downward spiral; the harder you try to break free, the more it pulls you to places, thoughts, or situations you would rather not be in. Not a very pleasant experience, is it?

Here's the big question: At what age did you start using and/or abusing on a regular basis? Think about it. Was it at age twelve, thirteen, nineteen, before then, after then? You decide, at what age was it? With that age in mind, I'll direct your attention back to the original question. At what age did you start regularly using and/or abusing? The truth is, your ability to cope with your feelings and emotions stopped maturing at the age your consecutive substance abuse began. It's very important that you understand what this means. I began abusing substances (cigarettes and beer) at about age eleven or twelve. I stopped my substance abuse, including intravenous drug use, using the Quick Fix techniques, in May 1987 at age twenty-eight. Much to my surprise, I found myself to be that age physically but only twelve or thirteen years old, at best, in regards to my coping mechanisms, feelings and emotions. I was very distressed with life, and found my responses to be like those of a teenager. Left to my own devices I was sure to perish. I didn't recover all by myself, and you don't have to either. We never have to do this alone, but it is so very important that you have a full understanding of this age issue. Now that we understand it, we must also accept it so we can move on.

Take heart. I have devised a system through which you can reestablish your abilities and learn to cope with life better than ever before. All it takes is time and persistent effort on your part to make

NOTE

www.bradleyquick.com

www.bradleyquick.com

NOTE
---

these wonderful changes in your life and the lives of those around you. You can do this! It's not an impossibility. This is a tried and proven method that works if you work it. All you must do is make the decision to work it. Make up your mind that you're so fed up with being sick and tired, that you're ready for positive change. What do fear and change have in common? Take a moment. That's right, they both involve the unknown. With change comes fear. That's one of the reasons why change is often times so very hard to initiate, much less to sustain over any period of time.

Change for us is usually only motivated by pain accompanied by complete mental and/or living chaos. Remember, if you keep doing what you're doing, you'll keep getting what you're getting. If you want something different, you have to do something different. The *Quick Fix Process* is your answer because it helps you to do something different than you've been doing. This method will broaden the spectrum through which you perceive yourself, your role and your objectives, as well as the objectives of others. This process will bring forth positive change to be admired by all, especially you. You must understand. We are individuals who have lost the ability to control the use of our substance(s), or participation in the disorders in question, and probably any other substance(s) or actions we may have shifted to in times of distress or condemnation.

Don't think for one moment that because you're having a hard time with scotch, you can just switch to vodka and everything will be OK, because it won't. It doesn't work that way. Nor can you switch from booze to pot, heroin to barbiturates, chocolate to caramel, Marlboros to Winston, French-fries to onion rings, or anything of the like. If you do, you are just shifting your addictive traits to another substance, and not progressing at all. And please don't get caught up in the anti-depressant game. My experience says if you do, you lose. I once knew a man who, after seven years of being substance abuse free, began to get very emotional, and for a time was unable to control his emotions, or reactions to outside stimuli. This man sought help for his current state of mind through the psychiatric profession. He was prescribed an anti-depressant, and some five years later, I witnessed this man on more than one occasion without his pills. He was a monster, a completely unpredictable lunatic. It would have been more advantageous for him to work through his uncomfortable state at seven years than to become strung out for a life-time on prescribed medications. Giving up one thing to become dependent on another doesn't make much sense, does it?

The real issue here is your lack of coping mechanisms and the substance(s) or behav-iors which you've substituted for those mech-anisms, so as to cope with this world and the people in it. You cannot afford to continue this way of living. You must remain abstinent from not only the behavior(s) in question, but from all related substances/disorders. No more using and/or abusing! If your abusive substance is a mind altering substance (alcohol, drugs, pot, etc.), you must completely avoid all substances that affect you from the neck up. If your substance is ciga-rettes, you must learn to avoid all tobaccos, pipes, cigars, nicotine, etc. If you have a food issue, by all means, stay away from fattening foods, sugars, starches, etc. (Consult your local dietary expert.) If it's a behavioral issue, follow this same process and be free. One is too many, a thousand never enough. Do not submit to the obsession and you will not be swept away.

Every single one of us that struggles with using and abusing behaviors was born with a personal radio station in our heads. Much of the time, the volume is high, at level 10. At other times, it's

NOTE

www.bradleyquick.com

www.bradleyquick.com

NOTE

lower, but it's always there. The programming on this station is always the same; self-sabotage, self-pity, obsession, drama, self-seeking, ego and fear. This is our own guilt and shame-based radio at its best. Here in California, a radio station's call letters always begin with a K, as in KNBC, KCBS, and so on. Our built-in substance abuse radio station that plays in our heads is commonly referred to as KFUK Self-Sabotage Radio. This is a joke that often seems so very real. Sometimes I begin to listen so intently to this programming, I start to believe it. It's at that time that I must stop and jump back into this *Quick Fix Process* in order to reexamine my perceptions. I must always remember that I don't have to listen to what my head is saying. I can, and do, simply reply aloud, "Thank you for sharing, now shut up." At times, that's all it takes. Other times, I find that when I extend myself to others it brings me much relief. Always be of service!

We are all good people. That's not the issue. We are in the grips of a progressive dilemma, using and abusing, which results in inappropriate actions. In my experience, for us, it only gets worse, never better. As soon as we accept that we must change, at least the destructive part of our lives, we begin to grow toward a better future, a better tomorrow. It's your life. The world revolves with you or without you, seasons will continue to change, the tides will continue to come and go. The world and everyone in it can get along just fine with or without you. This world has been around for billions of years. The universe will not miss you. So if you must continue, be my guest. If you're still thinking you can use your substance(s) or participate in your behaviors casually, I wish you all the luck in the world. My guess is you can't, you've tried. *So let's stop trying!* The deal I'm making with you is that you take this *Quick Fix* solution with you wherever you go. (Better to have it and not need it, than need it and not have it.) Apply the contents to every situation you encounter. You must listen to the *Positive Chat Power* CD (most important), and watch the positive change begin. Okay? Do we, you and I, have a deal or not? If we do, take a deep breath, and let the change begin. If not, you had better reevaluate your situation once again.

> *Remember, if you keep doing what you're doing, you'll keep getting what you're getting. If you want something different, you must do something different. No change, no gain.*

Here is your choice, so go ahead and make it now. Do you want to win or do you want to keep getting beaten by your abusive behaviors, your using and abusing? It's your decision!

Remember, self reliance is about as far as any of us ever got. An attitude of intolerance and indifference has generally been our code. Our best thinking got us into this mess, so let's not rely on ourselves to fix it. Let's rely on this process. It works, it really does. Though it's not easy, it's well worth it. So let's do it together. Let's consider this getting C.L.E.A.N. (Clearly Learning Everything Absolutely Necessary) from unsatisfactory behaviors and/or using and abusing substances.

> Thought: *You're only as positive, or as negative, as the atmosphere you're in, and only as positive or as negative as the company you keep!*

This is not about race or family of origin. It's about freedom from substance abuse and behavioral disorders. It's about being happy and contented with life. Together we can stay free from using and abusing, alone we fall right back into destruction. *Fact:* If anyone else would have done the things to me that I've done to myself, I would have bopped them a long time ago. If you can be honest with

NOTE

www.bradleyquick.com

51

_____
NOTE
_____

yourself, I'm sure you can make the same statement. I'm willing to bet that in your entire life, you were never your own best friend because you didn't respect yourself. That's how I was. Let's not depend on ourselves, but go through this process together. We can support each other and not have to be out there alone. Let's get started.

www.bradleyquick.com

The Guarantee

If you don't put forth any effort into this *Quick Fix Process,* I can personally guarantee you bad results. You might as well give this program away now; just make sure you give it to someone in need of solutions in their life. On the other hand, if you put forth, say, 50% effort, you can expect only minimal results, if any at all. You will get out of this only what you put into it, no more, no less. That's my guarantee to you. This is a sure winner, no ifs, ands or buts. This will work for you if you will work it. Let's not be foolish. We're talking about your life and your well being, not a laughing matter at all. At this moment, the most important person on the face of the planet is reading this sentence, but if that very important person, you, doesn't follow this simple process, you will remain the same, get worse, or maybe even, from time to time, wish you were dead. Your options after reading this handbook and failing to follow through with the process will be limited to feeling like you do today. You may even wind up in jail, a mental institutions or die. That's where people like you and me end up. Is this something to look forward to? I think not.

My guarantee is that you'll get out of this exactly what you put into it, no more, no less. However, if you give this all you've got, wondrous things will begin to happen to you, and for you, in your life. That's the guarantee. You might just lose your need to always be right. You may suddenly gain a new freedom and a new happiness, and a willingness to help others. Your attitude and outlook in regard to life will definitely change for the better. Selfish,

www.bradleyquick.com

www.bradleyquick.com

NOTE

self-seeking behavior may vanish and be substituted by a true desire to help others and, when needed, to share your firsthand experience with them. You will no longer have fear of those you admire and/or those with authority. You will only have occasional, if any, episodes of financial insecurity, and you will come to realize it's never as bad as we think it is.

Once you are substance abuse and behavioral disorder free, you will recognize that you have always had, and shall always have, enough to get by, even if getting by doesn't meet our current expectations. Whatever the situation, despite the expectations, you will have enough. You have found a new purpose in life. One that's being discovered more profoundly every day as we swing at the pitches life throws us with the clarity needed to avoid the bad pitches and hit the good ones right out of the park. As you gain clarity, your perception becomes less distorted, and your desire to be someone you are not will begin to fade away. You will become eager to embrace the opportunities to be all that you can and will be. Life's peaks and valleys will never disappear; it's our living equilibrium that gets better. We are better equipped intuitively to handle all that life deals us, and when we don't have the answer, or know the solution, we don't hesitate to ask someone and to be humble in receiving their answer.

If these facts are appealing to you, as I think they may be, then you should not hesitate for a moment to indulge yourself in this process. Take advantage of the simplicity of the required daily actions that will invoke such a profound change in your life, your existence, and your well-being.

Today, I'm the best me I've ever been. Sure, there are good days and bad days, everyone has them, but all in all I've never had it so good. I've got the house, the clothes, the car, and all that stuff on the outside. That's a given. I've also received, more times than not, inner peace, tranquility, serenity and soundness of mind. And in those moments of self-obsession, I know where to turn. I don't hesitate for one moment to reach out and ask for help, clarification, and understanding. I'm healthy and physically fit. I am a desirable individual to be – at least with most of the time!

Remember, we all have our bad moments. I, too, have experienced pain and adversity, homelessness and lack of health, while being and remaining substance abuse free. There is no reason in the world, not one, to abandon these principles and this process for the sake of your disorders just because tough times arise. Yet it happens all the time. People get clean and sober, substance abuse and behavioral disorder free, forget where they came from, and stop doing all the things that saved them in the first place. Do you know what happens then? You guessed it, they go right back from where they came, and more times than not, it's at a much quicker, more severe pace. They find themselves worse off than ever, more hopeless and helpless than before. Some of us even die as a result.

> You will have your tough moments. Life is not all bliss for anyone, but you will have a process to get through any and all that comes across your path, if you do what it takes *Just Right Now* to stay substance abuse and behavioral disorder free. By resolving your issues with clarity of mind, you will only get better at coping with all issues that come your way, in all aspects of your life. That's the **guarantee**!

www.bradleyquick.com

The Seven Stages of Development

1. Denial *(Not me)* Substance abuse and behavioral disorders are the only afflictions I know that will allow you to believe that you're not afflicted at all, and to deny it if ever confronted, even if help is being offered to you gently with genuine kindness and concern. "Don't confuse me with the facts, my mind is made up," is our response when we are in denial. Denial is the enemy. It prevents growth of any kind. Denying this issue in your life is the same as if you had cancer and the medical community told you that there was a cure. With that information in mind, you just continued along like there was no problem. When all you had to do is to follow a simple process to the best of your ability—just for right now, in this moment—to be free from cancer. Why would you not surrender to the cure? Substance abuse and/or behavioral disorders at this time is your cancer and this is your cure. If you'll do what it takes, just in this moment, with this *Quick Fix Process,* you will be free. Stay out of denial!

2. Acceptance *(I'm alright)* Acceptance is the key to all of our problems today. Acknowledging this is to accept ourselves, and our current circumstances and conditions. In order to move on, we must first acknowledge the problem, then accept what is. Total acceptance is always accompanied by a sigh of relief as the weight of the world is lifted off your shoulders and you finally realize you're free to begin again. Acceptance is the key.

www.bradleyquick.com

3. Surrender *(I give up)* You have now made a decision to relinquish control, to give it back to the universe and all its inhabitants and to let what is, be what it is at any given moment. With this surrender comes a newfound freedom, and as long as you continue this process daily, you will remain on top of the proverbial pink cloud. Enjoy letting go!

4. Willingness *(Positive action)* You now have a newfound willingness to do whatever it takes to enhance positive change in your life, your situation, the lives of others and in this, your new growth process. The more efforts you put forth, the more profound the growth. The more profound your growth, the more you benefit yourself and the world. Just be willing to be willing and let the universe do its thing.

5. Depression *(Complacency)* After a time, we once again start to participate in life and tend to forget from whence we came. As we resume our life, we find ourselves with more important things to do than what has been required thus far to get us to this point of self discovery/recovery. As life gets more comfortable and we get more complacent, we start to compare ourselves to those that have what we want or think we should have. Reality sets in as to who we are and who we are not, often much to our surprise. The complications of life begin to mount, and again we forget what we did to get here. The manure hits the fan! Don't get discouraged. This is only part of your natural evolution, and with the proper action, this too shall pass (P.A.C.E.). I promise. Remember, it's easier to act yourself into positive thinking, than to think yourself into positive action.

www.bradleyquick.com

www.bradleyquick.com

NOTE

6. More Willingness *(Positive action resumes)* Being in so much pain at this point, you'll realize you've got only two choices. The first is to go back to substances or behavioral disorders hoping to relieve the pain. The second choice is to immediately resume the actions that brought you freedom and comfort when you first started working this process. One is an option and the other a death sentence. Good luck, and don't forget to seek, read, and then follow direction.

7. Maturity *(Self-acceptance)* It's been a long hard road up to this point. Growing up is never easy to do, but it's starting to pay off. You know more or less who you are. You pretty much know who you want to be when you grow up. You now realize you never have to do this thing called life alone, and that you have an active role in the lives of many. Helen Keller once wrote, "Through my greatest handicap I have found my god, my work, and my purpose." At this point, maybe you feel the same way. If not, stay focused on this process and it will come.

Congratulations and welcome aboard.

> Remember, the closer you stay to this process *the better you will feel and the better life will be. The further you drift away, the rougher the road gets and the harder the climb back.*

My firsthand experience indicates that there is generally no time schedule associated with these stages of recovery. They are all related to your current efforts, perceptions and frame of mind. Let these stages, 1 through 7, act as your guide to get from where you are to where you want to be. Naturally, the more profound your experience in each stage, the more longevity it will have as you take it into the next stages of your evolution.

CHAPTER 7

Making Things Up

"I think my mate is cheating on me." Could this assessment be just a lack of self-esteem on your part, is your faulty perception a proverbial reading between the lines, or are you just making things up? A lot of people in this world, including myself on occasion, have a tendency to make things up whether out of fear, self-preservation, looking good, or just trying not to look so bad. We invent better scenarios.

On one occasion, while living with a girl in Spokane, Washington, I had built such a case against this young lady (my fears) in my head throughout the day that, when I got home she didn't have a chance. There she was relaxed on the couch in a sexy nightgown, pleasantly welcoming me home, and I blew up at this girl. She didn't have a prayer. She was ambushed, and all she did was have a meal and open arms waiting for me, and still she got that type of reaction from me. The point being, out of my jealous fear (lack of self-esteem and self-worth) and my fear of being abandoned, she didn't have a chance. While away from her during the day, I had, in my mind, made up and believed that she was seeing someone else, that her plans did not include me, and other perceived betrayals. This was not really happening anywhere but between my ears. It started with only a tiny jealous thought (a fear), and ended up being my entire mindset and focus. Just as every time before, when I made things up, I believed them and lived them, always ending up regretting the outcomes that resulted from my thoughts, from the "my mind's made up" delusions I harbored.

NOTE

www.bradleyquick.com

NOTE

You've heard the term, "Don't confuse me with the facts. My mind's made up." We are the perfect example of that very saying. We have been, are still are, unwilling to let the truth prevail, because it might blemish our character, when in fact, we could not look sillier than standing our ground with our arms crossed. Yet we persist in holding onto our foolish, self-delusional pride. Figure that one out.

So I must look for and accept what really is and not read between the lines and/or make things up. That is so easy to do, but I must do all I can to avoid it for my own well-being, as well as the well being of others. If ever I do unintentionally make something up (and this will happen from time to time), I can correct it on the spot or, if after the fact I make this realization, I can always go back and fess up as to my error (see *Amends* in the Glossary section of this book).

You may have been in an elevator sometime and seen someone very appealing, someone you might like to meet and then before the elevator doors open, in your head, you've already been married, divorced, and in a custody battle for the children with that person, and now are glad you didn't say anything. In fact, your fellow passenger may have been the "one", but because of your warped thinking, you'll never know. *(KFUK, Self-Sabotage Radio)*

Positive Chat Power

Listening to the *Positive Chat Power* CD's is definitely one of the most important aspects of this process. While you're consciously working this process on a daily basis, the *Positive Chat Power* recorded messages are going back stage, into your subconscious mind, negotiating a better deal for you. Since these recordings are talking to the boss directly (your subconscious mind), they will get much faster and more profound results than will negotiation with the conscious mind. A bigger and faster payoff for you!

Voila, you are now enhancing your mind's acceptance and application of this information by as much as a few hundred times. If that's not an easier, softer way to instill positive change, then I doubt one exists. There is no faster way to absorb change from within one's self than through *Positive Chat Power*. There just isn't. If there was I would have found it by now. I've sure looked into several different methods and in my opinion there's just no faster way to implement change, period.

Here's the theory behind *Positive Chat Power*. The mind is divided into three sections:
1. The conscious mind
2. The critical mind
3. The subconscious mind

The conscious mind is about 12% of the brain. This is where all the analytical processes are made such as thoughts, fears, decisions, judgments, etc. The Critical mind acts as a gatekeeper by dividing the conscious mind and the subconscious mind. The subconscious mind is about 88% of the brain and executes the internal programming, without

www.bradleyquick.com

www.bradleyquick.com

NOTE

judgment, without fear, without hesitation, and it does this 24 hours a day, 7 days a week, 365 days a year, for your entire life. It even works while you're sleeping (we know these as dreams.)

There once was a movie *2001: A Space Odyssey*. If you have seen it, you may remember that in the movie there was a computer they called Hal. Hal ran the spaceship. Hal had the ability and control to override anything and anybody at almost anytime. Hal finally went crazy and destroyed not only the ship and the crew, but eventually himself as well. With an unfavorable program, even a machine can only glide through space for so long. How long do you think a fragile, vulnerable human being with an unfavorable program can last?

Your subconscious mind is much the same as Hal. Once self-sabotage sets in and the self-destruct mode takes over, it's all over for us unless we implement change from within. *We must change our internal programming for the better from within.*

Understand first that your subconscious mind is full of "knowns" (familiar things) and "unknowns" (things not familiar). These "knowns" and "unknowns" are not necessarily good or bad, right or wrong, ethical or unethical. They are just the things that your subconscious mind has come to know during your early years (birth to twelve) as being acceptable to you or unacceptable for you.

Thus our homeostasis is born; our interests, our likes and dislikes, what we'll accept and won't accept, how we'll act and react to various external and internal stimuli, and so on. This is the basis of our character, our personality. The job of the critical mind (the gatekeeper) is to allow only the current known information through and into the subconscious mind, and to keep all the unknowns out. This is attempted self-preservation by your inner program. Now, if our self-preservation, or conditioned interpretations and responses, are regulated only by our misinterpretation of our perceived reality, then our self-preservation reactions may be even more detrimental to our well being than would an unhampered true response. Because of our mind's not knowing how to react or respond we often react inappropriately, thus creating an uncomfortable and/or embarrassing predicament.

Example: We have two armies, both have the same weapons. However, one army has twelve soldiers and the other eight-eight soldiers. Who is the most likely to be the victor of every battle? Not a difficult a question, but yes, the largest army wins every time. We'll call the smaller army your conscious mind. It often has brilliant strategies (good intent) and excellent marksmanship (good reasoning) and will sometimes give the bigger army, your subconscious mind, a run for the money. Yet, the larger army, your subconscious mind, always wins. So what we must do is infiltrate the subconscious mind with new plans, motives and ideas, with purpose and ambitions for positive change. Together, we can do that! We can reprogram your subconscious mind for positive change, and as a result, you win. This is not an overnight process, but bet on yourself in this race, because if you stay on course you're going to win. Every time!

You see through *Positive Chat Power,* we can make new and better "knowns" for you, and change some of your current "knowns" (negative habits, thoughts, motives, and desires) to "unknowns," thus changing your subconscious mind's perceived input, desired output, and results.

The fact is, by using this *Positive Chat Power Process*, together we can go through the conscious mind, overpower the gatekeeper, and move straight into the subconscious mind with positive inspiration. Then, by altering the believability and receptiveness to suggestion by your subconscious mind, we create magic (change), and miracles will happen for you, again and again.

NOTE

www.bradleyquick.com

www.bradleyquick.com

NOTE

Believe it or not, you alternate between your conscious mind and subconscious mind all day long. It's just not purposely guided. I'm sure you have, at one time or another, been driving down the highway, going someplace you've been to many times before, and completely missed the intended exit. We've all done that. That's a perfect example of being in a subconscious state. Your conscious mind was overloaded and your subconscious mind was interpreting and reacting to everything. You didn't get in an accident, you didn't hurt yourself, you could hear, you could see, and before you knew it, once again, you became consciously aware and went on about your business. (Probably, while turning around and either laughing at or cursing at yourself for missing the exit.) No harm, no foul. Let *Positive Chat Power* change your life!

To download the complete *Positive Chat Power* CD series, (download *Positive Chat Power* CD 1 FREE), or any individual programs, at $4.95 each visit www.positivechatpower.com
Or send check or money order
for $9.95 each (plus $7.00 S&H)
to: The Cool Change Foundation, Inc.
PO Box 160 North Hollywood CA 91603

Overcoming Addictions	Finding Inner Peace
Stopping Self-sabotage	Increasing Self-esteem
Eliminating Fear & Anxiety	Inner Child, Happy Past!
Acceptance, Making Life Easy	Enhancing Self Confidence
Instant Stress Relief	Relaxation Techniques
Maximizing Motivation	Weight Loss Motivation

12 Life Changing Programs

The *"Positive Chat Power"*(guided meditation) CD series enhances, then solidifies the positive behaviors that are part of the solution. The *Positive Chat Power* recorded suggestions are building blocks to making permanent changes. These positive building blocks improve every aspect of your life through the following programs:

Overcoming Addictions
Finding Inner Peace
Stopping Self-sabotage
Increasing Self-esteem
Eliminating Fear & Anxiety
Inner Child, Happy Past!
Acceptance, Making Life Easy
Enhancing Self Confidence
Instant Stress Relief
Relaxation Techniques
Maximizing Motivation
Weight Loss Motivation

If you will accept this *Positive Chat Power* approach for what it really is, it will work for you. You'll feel better than before, I promise, you really will. In these life changing messages, you will learn how to attain a state of positive, powerful inspiration and how to relax and let your natural mind go to work for you, so that you, too, can achieve more positive and more profound results in your life, relationships, and goals.

Naturally, positive actions and reactions, or positive automatic conditioned responses from within, will be yours by simply utilizing this method. To start, listen to or read the *Getting Started with Positive Chat Power CD 1* two days in a row, one time per day. That's once a day for two days in a row, then as needed over time, to attain a stronger and deeper state of Inspiration. After ordering the rest of the *Positive Chat Power CD*

www.bradleyquick.com

www.bradleyquick.com

——————— NOTE ———————

series, for best results, you should only listen to one *Positive Chat Power* message per day to attain the strongest state of inspired thought. Each *Positive Chat Power* message in this series should be listened to seven times in a row. That means listen to the same *Positive Chat Power* message on seven separate occasions in a row before moving on to the next message in the series. Each message in this series will enhance a different positive aspect of your character. I suggest you find a very comfortable place to sit and relax while listening to these life changing messages.

These CDs are not to be listened to while driving or operating any type of vehicle or machinery. Best results will be achieved while listening in a quiet, safe place.

Getting Started with Positive Chat Power:

Example induction into Positive Chat Power

So, now I want you to nuzzle your body into a comfortable position, whether that's lying down, or sitting in the reclined position. It's very important at this time to just get comfortable.

Let's first understand that *Positive Chat Power* is a tool used to create a suggestible receptor in the mind allowing you to rid yourself of inhibitions or habits that maybe holding you back in life. *Positive Chat Power* also allows you to relax, feel more comfortable and inspired. During and after this process, tensions and pressures of the day, the week, the month and the year will start to disappear. Through this *Positive Chat Power* series, concentration and mental alertness are heightened, you are more alert mentally and your senses are more acute.

Positive Chat Power is a combination of words. As you know, words can affect us to the point where they can make us angry or sleepy. They can stimulate all the sensations in our body. We can, through words, feel heaviness or lightness, extreme heat or cold. Now through these *Positive Chat Power* words, you can expect drowsiness and relaxation to take place. As you enter an inspired state, certain physical changes begin to take hold.

You will notice your breathing becoming deep, gentle, and rhythmic. Your lips and throat might become dry, and you will have the urge to swallow. You'll be aware of, but you'll pay no attention to, any outside sounds, just my voice, for these outside sounds are everyday sounds of life and cannot distract or disturb you. They will tend to relax you, and allow you to go even deeper into this deep, heavy concentration.

At this time, allow your eyes to close, as your body and your mind begin to relax. There you go, let yourself begin to hear my voice as you start to relax. Now as your breathing deepens, I will direct your attention to your mind. With your eyes closed, focus all your attention on your mind, and let it relax. Realize that now your mind is beginning to relax. As your breathing deepens, you notice that every breath you inhale brings you complete and total relaxation, and with every breath you exhale, you're able to release the stress, worry, and anxiety leaving your body. There you go. Every breath you take in brings you more relaxation as your mind continues to relax. Now breathe deep, as you focus on relaxing your mind. There you are, just let the stress, worry, and concern in your mind go. That's it.

As your mind now relaxes even more, let's focus on relaxing your brain. Let the warm, flowing sense of relaxation flow from your mind into your brain. There you go, now your brain begins to relax. With every breath you take in, your brain relaxes even

NOTE

www.bradleyquick.com

www.bradleyquick.com

NOTE

more. Now your mind and your brain are beginning to relax as you feel that warm, flowing sense of relaxation starting to flow from your mind to your brain, and now downward even further into your forehead. There you go, let your forehead relax. All the worry, concern, stress, and anxiety of the day, the week, the month, and the year is now leaving your forehead as you begin and continue to relax. There you go. As your breathing deepens, you can now feel that warm, flowing sense of relaxation moving down through your body, as it flows from your mind, into your brain, into your forehead, and now down into your eyes.

Deep breath. Your eyes now relax, and they may have a tendency to roll back up into your head, and that's all right, just let them go. Deep breath, as that warm, flowing sense of relaxation now moves from your mind, into your brain, into your forehead, down into your eyes and now down into your jaw. That's it, let the warm, smooth relaxation flow through your body, as your jaw muscles begin to relax, all the stress is now being released from all the relaxed parts of your body including your jaw. Let it go. As that warm, flowing sense of relaxation now flows from your jaw down into your upper neck. Feel your upper neck relax, as all the worry, concern, stress and anxiety being stored in the muscles of your upper neck are now leaving. All the stress being stored in your upper, mid and lower back is now leaving, gone with every breath.

That's right. Go ahead, breath deep, breath in the relaxation, exhale all the stress, worry, and concern of the day, the week, the month and the year. That's right, now just allow your body to relax, as that warm, flowing sense of relaxation now flows from, and into your mind, your brain, your forehead, your eyes, your jaw and your upper neck down into your lower neck and shoulders. As your lower neck and shoulders begin to relax, you are feeling an incredible warm sense of relaxation. Breathing becomes very deep, gentle, and rhythmic, and the drowsy, sleepy, daydreaming, a feeling of relaxation takes over. You're letting go . . . drifting down deeper and deeper, as the warm, flowing sense of relaxation continues to flow through your body. From your neck and shoulders, down into your chest and stomach area, as your entire body becomes saturated with relaxation. As this relaxation becomes heavier and heavier, as this warm, flowing sense of relaxation moves down from your chest and stomach into your waist, your hips, your thighs, into your knees, calves, ankles, feet and toes. You begin to relax your entire body, feeling that warm sense of relaxation flow from your shoulders to your biceps, into your triceps, forearms, wrists hands and fingers. You may feel a numb, pleasant, tingling sensation through your fingers and toes, as this relaxation grows deeper and deeper.

Now, as I count down from five to zero, each count will represent deep relaxation, and you will feel your body relaxing even more as I count down and you let yourself go. Deeper and deeper, and when I reach zero, you will go deep asleep. Now let yourself go with . . . five . . . four . . . letting go . . . three . . . going deeper . . . two . . . one . . . zero . . . (snap your fingers) deep sleep . . . deep sleep . . . that's right... complete and total relaxation.

Now concentrate on my voice and you will go even more deeply asleep with every breath that you exhale. From this point on, every time I count down from five to zero, zero being deep sleep, you will reach this level of concentration, quickly, soundly, and deeply. Quickly soundly and deeply. As you have now entered an inspired state, you can rest assured that we are only going on a relaxing, fun loving, guided journey, one that will result in your positive evolution.

NOTE
_____

www.bradleyquick.com

www.bradleyquick.com

_____
NOTE
_____

Now, take a deep breath, and be willing to accept this positive change into your life now. At this time, I would like you to completely let go, and imagine that you are falling. Falling backwards into space, just relax and fall, that's it. Let yourself go. Falling, falling, falling, let go, that's it. Let yourself fall safely backwards into your inner universe. That's it. That's it. Let go now.

Now in your mind, you will repeat after me:

I am open to all possibilities before me and know that only good can result from changing.

I respect myself now, which gives me courage to further change and grow.

I accept my past and see how it has shaped my life today.

I am now able to stay in the moment.

I accept good into my life and welcome it when it comes.

I am grateful for my life and my experiences.

I am now willing to let go of all unnecessary fear in my life.

I am now willing to let go of all anxiety in my life.

I am not fearful or anxious now or anytime.

I now replace all unnecessary fear with joy and happiness.

I now replace all unnecessary anxiety with joy and happiness.

I am more times than not full of joy and happiness.

I embrace change and accept it as a necessary part of my growth and expansion.

I allow myself to prosper by experiencing completion in all my affairs.

I have the resources to handle whatever happens in my life without experiencing fear or anxiety.

Today I make loving choices for myself and accept good into my life.

I am committed to taking positive actions that will move my projects along today.

I forgive those that hurt me, because they are in pain.

I am now able to stay in the moment.

I accept the guidance from my heart and handle my affairs with honesty.

I accept new good into my life and welcome it when it comes.

I am now willing to let go of all unnecessary fear in my life.

I am now willing to let go of all anxiety in my life.

NOTE

www.bradleyquick.com

_____ NOTE _____

www.bradleyquick.com

I am not fearful or anxious now or anytime.

I now replace all unnecessary fear with joy and happiness.

I now replace all anxiety with joy and happiness.

I find that I am able to stay in the moment.

I am more often than not full of joy and happiness.

I am compassionate and loving to myself in everyway.

Today I let go of my perfectionism so that I can participate more in the excitement of life.

Today I allow the excitement of change to fill my life.

Today I see beyond my fear and live a joyous, prosperous life.

Today I release the fear that keeps me from moving on.

I respect the power of words in creating my reality.

Today I am responsible for taking good care of myself.

Today I let go of resentments that keep me away from my greater good.

Today I open my heart to the abundance around me.

Today I have the ability to say "no" when it's appropriate.

I am grateful for my life and my experiences.

Today I acknowledge my fear and anxiety but go beyond it.

Today I let go of painful experiences and understand what purpose they serve in my growth process.

Today I walk through my fear by taking action toward achieving my goals.

I receive from my senses and experience the intimacy of the moment.

Today I have enough time to take care of what I need to do.

Now take a deep breath, and know this is all about positive change for you, and your willingness to accept this positive change into your life now. I would like you to completely let go, and imagine that you are falling. Falling backwards into space. That's it. Let yourself go. Falling, falling, falling, let go, that's it. Let yourself fall safely backwards into your dark, black, inner universe. That's it. That's it. Let's go now.

Now imagine you have landed, and you are now lying on your back, feeling nothing but love and the nice, cool breeze blowing across your face. Embrace the feeling. Now, in your mind, open your eyes, look up, and find yourself under a big tree. It's a beautiful tree, lots of branches, very full and green, and you begin to hear the birds chirping, as

---

NOTE

www.bradleyquick.com

www.bradleyquick.com

NOTE

you look up through the tree and see the beautiful blue sky above. Now you lean up onto your elbows and forearms to find that you are on the side of a hill, surrounded by tall green grass, and you notice that cool breeze blowing through the tall grass. And you look up to find white powder puff clouds in the deep blue sky above. To your right, off in the distance, you see a stream flowing down the hill. As your eyes follow the stream down the hill to the bottom of the valley, you see a big lake, a big beautiful blue lake with clear water surrounded by big beautiful trees. As you look across the lake, you see on the other side, a log cabin with a chimney sticking up. There is smoke rising out of that chimney, and as you now take a deep breath, you can smell fresh cut wood that must be burning in the fireplace. You feel very fresh and relaxed now, under this tree, on the hillside, among the tall green wind blown grass.

And as you sit up, you now focus your attention up to the top of the hill. You see a faint image coming over the hill, the image of a little person out in the distance walking down the hill. You watch as this small person, off in the distance, gets closer and approaches the stream that runs down the hill. And as this small person climbs down to the side of the stream, you see this person jump over the stream and move across some rocks, getting closer and closer, coming down the hill and moving towards you. You may now begin to think you recognize this small person, but you can't yet distinguish the face, as the small image gets closer and closer to you. Let's wait a moment as this small person approaches.

Now, if you haven't already done so, go ahead and reach out for their small hand as it becomes very clear who this little person is. You realize you know this small person very well, but it has been such a long time. Go ahead now, get close if you desire. You may want to hug or hold each other, or just be there. You know that you have so much to catch up on. Why don't the two of you take a moment for yourselves and do what you feel like doing and I'll be quiet for a moment.

Hello again. I know that there's so much to say and so little time, but you can come back to this place, whenever you like, I promise! However, it's now time to say goodbye to your little person, and as you let go, know deep inside that you will see this person again soon. If you have not done so already, look at this person now and say your good-byes. And as you watch this small person climb up the hill towards the stream, you know that you can and will benefit from this meeting. As they climb over the rocks, and jump over the stream, it's up to the top of the hill they go.

Now you see them off in the distance as they stop, turn around, and wave at you. And now that little image begins to fade and disappears over the hill. You now turn around and sit, again noticing the breeze as it blows the tall grass on the hillside, noticing the deep blue sky above with the powder puff clouds. And as you again, looking across the valley, you see the big crystal clear lake and the log cabin with the smoking chimney, as you again take a deep breath, smelling the firewood and once again beginning to relax. You decide to lie down again, under the big beautiful tree, getting comfortable, hearing the birds and looking through the branches at the blue sky. Deep Breath.

Now, in your mind, close your eyes, and again, you begin to fall backwards. Falling free into the inner space of your mind, falling, falling, let yourself go. That's right, safely falling, completely free. There you go, just let it happen. Pause, deep breath.

You have now, once again, arrived back to where you started. You are now back in the same place where you began listening to this message, again feeling the sensations in your hands and

NOTE

www.bradleyquick.com

www.bradleyquick.com

NOTE

fingers, once again being aware of the sounds around you, taking only the good from this experience and leaving the rest. Again, concentrate on my voice, and know from this point on, every time you hear my voice counting down from five to zero, zero being deep sleep, you will reach this level of inspiration, quickly, soundly, and deeply. Quickly–soundly–and deeply. In a few moments, I will count upwards from zero to five. Five, always represents a fully awakened state, physically relaxed, emotionally calm, intellectually alert and fully awake. Here we go. Coming back.

Zero . . . one . . . two . . . feeling good . . .three . . . refreshed and energetic . . .beginning to smile . . . four . . .can't ' hold the smile back . . . five . . .yes open!. Wide awake! . . . one . . .two . . . three . . . four . . . five . . .eyes open, wide awake!

Congratulations! You have just contributed to, and participated in, your own positive evolution. Remember, listen to or read this message, *Getting Started with Positive Chat Power*, twice. That's once per day, for two days straight. NOW GO AND INSPIRE THE WORLD!

To download the complete *Positive Chat Power* CD series, (download *Positive Chat Power* CD 1 FREE), or any individual programs, at $4.95 each visit www.positivechatpower.com Or send check or money order for $9.95 each (plus$7.00 S&H) to: The Cool Change Foundation, Inc. PO Box 160 North Hollywood CA 91603

Overcoming Addictions	Finding Inner Peace
Stopping Self-sabotage	Increasing Self-esteem
Eliminating Fear & Anxiety	Inner Child, Happy Past!
Acceptance, Making Life Easy	Enhancing Self Confidence
Instant Stress Relief	Relaxation Techniques
Maximizing Motivation	Weight Loss Motivation

Needs

Neurotransmitters

www.bradleyquick.com

CONCORDANCE   www.bradleyquick.com

B. Listen to *Positive Chat Power*. To start; **download FREE or order Getting Started** with *Positive Chat Power* CD 1 program for you and your personal development. You should not delay in ordering or downloading *Positive Chat Power but ABSOLUTELY DO NOT postpone your participation in the rest of The Quick Fix process just because you don't have Positive Chat Power yet. Remember, positive action cures everything!* However, when you receive your download or CD(s) begin by listening, **quiet and alone (not while driving)**, to any one program daily for at least 7 consecutive days before moving on to the next program. Do listen daily! The more the subconscious mind (your inner program) takes in, the faster the results. These results will be a newfound assortment of coping mechanisms and abilities once nonexistent to you (***Automatic Conditioned Responses***). There is no easier way to get started and to sustain your newfound freedom. Additional recorded sessions include, but are not limited to:

    Overcoming Addictions
    Maximizing Motivation
    Increasing Self-Esteem
    Acceptance, Making Life Easy
    Relaxation Techniques
    Enhancing Self Confidence

Listen to the same message for at least 7 consecutive days. Listen, quiet and alone, listen over and over and over again. Start out listening daily (the more the subconscious mind takes in, the faster the results), though never listen any less than three times per week. Repetition will create automatic conditioned responses from within. There is no easier way to get started and to sustain your newfound freedom.

C. Review every morning. Spend 10 minutes every morning rereading your handbook highlights, doing your *Affirmations*, reading the *Quick 10*, and believing that you can. The longer

NOTE

www.bradleyquick.com

www.bradleyquick.com

and the more study put forth, the better, but a minimum of 10 minutes per day is necessary for positive change.

D. Exercise daily. Exercise your body at least once per day. Walk, jog, bike, swim, do aerobics or lift weights. Break a sweat, you'll feel better and your entire perception of life will change. (Consult your doctor before beginning any rigorous physical activity.) Remember to stretch before and after exercise (see Stretching).

E. Schedule. Write yourself a daily schedule. Before you start your day, review what you need and wish to get done on this day. First, make a list of the things you would like to accomplish today, and also those things that you must get done before the day is over. Then simply associate those tasks with a time of day, and go for it! No more thinking to it, now it's time to just go do it. One of the men I mentor once said to me, "I don't like thinking about what I should do next so I just do the next task on my schedule." For him, it meant that he didn't have to think about what task he was to do next, he just followed his list of what needed to be done and did it! Not much to think about!

F. Suit up, show up, put one foot in front of the other. Today, just do the job that's put in front of you to the best of your ability and stay out of the results. Remember, you are in the efforts business, not the results business. Stay out of expectations, it only brings with it disappointment.

G. Be Willing. Ask yourself throughout the day for the willingness to be honest and humble and that your motives not be selfish or self-seeking. Just for today, stay out of self-pity, be willing to act more instinctively without your analyzing thought processes. Carry this handbook with you and refer to it (*Glossary, Checklist, Highlights, Affirmations*, etc.) as needed throughout your day. Better to have it and not need it than need it and not have it.

H. Call for help. It's always most beneficial to get another opinion from somebody involved in this process before taking any impulsive action. If you have someone close to you that understands you and the *Quick Fix Process,* by all means, contact them first. If not, call the Help Line. Don't hesitate, do one or the other immediately. (Please see the Reference section for additional support groups.)

I. Getting Ready for Sleep. Before sleeping, reread your handbook highlights, do your *Affirmations* and don't forget to write your *Daily Journal* entry. If you've had a challenging or confrontational day, you should be sure to refer to *Resentments* in the *Glossary* or *Daily Journal* section. Make sure to work the simple but beneficial process found there for immediate and lasting relief of all those daily anxieties, grudges and challenging issues. It only works if you work it!

J. Make up your mind. Make up your mind that tomorrow will be a better day than today. You have learned through your experience today how to be a better you tomorrow. It's only a mistake if we don't learn from it, and simply a lesson if we take it for what it is, learn from it, and move on. Don't think for a minute you're unable to do this. Just become willing to become willing, and watch the magic unfold. Don't doubt what you can accomplish here. Remember, self-doubt is an illusion, an incorrect perception of yourself. You cannot allow yourself to be the judge of who you are or what you do Though this process is slow, it's also a sure thing. Slow but sure, and you can do it. What a relief!

K. Read *The Quick 10.* Read *The Quick 10* daily (the next section), at least once.

NOTE

www.bradleyquick.com

www.bradleyquick.com

NOTE	# The Quick 10

Just for Today I will try to live through this day only one moment at a time, and not try to tackle all my problems at once. I'm capable of doing something for a few hours that would appall me if I thought I had to keep it up for a lifetime. So I certainly can live in, and for, today.

Just for Today I will be happy. Abraham Lincoln once said that, "Most folks are as happy as they make up their minds to be." Today I have made up my mind to be happy!

Just for Today I will alter myself to what is, and not try to adjust everything to fit my own desires. I will take life as it comes and fit myself to it.

Just for Today I will try to strengthen my body and mind. I will study something useful, and I will exercise. I will not be a mental loafer or a couch potato. I will do something that requires effort, thought and concentration.

Just for Today I will exercise my soul in three ways: I will do someone a good turn and not tell anyone about it. If anyone knows of it, it will not count. I will do at least two things I don't want to do, just for good measure. I will not show anyone that my feelings are hurt. They may be hurt, but today I will not show it.

Just for Today I will be agreeable. I will look as well as I can, dress becomingly, keep my voice low, be courteous and not criticize. I will not find fault with anyone or anything, nor try to improve nor regulate anyone but myself.

Just for Today I will work this process. I may not follow it exactly, but I will work it to the best of my ability. I will save myself from two pests: *hurry and indecision.*

Just for Today I will have a quiet half-hour all by myself, and relax. During this half-hour, I will try to get a better perspective of my life.

Just for Today I will be unafraid. I will especially not be afraid to enjoy what is beautiful and to believe that as *I give to the world, so the world will give to me.*

Just for Today I will put my best efforts forward in all I do. I will stay out of the results and acknowledge that today I am in the efforts business, not the results business.

The more willingness you have, the more trust you gain, and the more trust you gain, the more willingness you have. Your reliance on this process will grow as your trust in this process grows. What we have here is a daily reprieve contingent on the maintenance of this process. Love and tolerance of others is now our key. Love brings with it some wonderful attributes, two of them being compassion and understanding. Our own circle of humanity will be better as a result of us possessing those attributes.

Tolerance brings with it self-containment and discipline, two things most of us are notorious for not having enough of. We will be better individuals, both inside and out, by practicing self-containment and discipline throughout our day. I can personally guarantee this. The other side of the coin is that you can always be in fear and attempted control. Just beware, as fear and control bring with them disappointment, envy, hate, and rage, none of which are very comfortable, or appealing.

NOTE

www.bradleyquick.com

87

www.bradleyquick.com

NOTE

Again it's your choice: Love and tolerance, or fear and control? Using the *Quick Fix Process*, you can learn to make the right decision. Make the choice that will best benefit you and your loved ones. This process is very simple, so keep it that way, don't complicate it. This process gives you daily rituals that bring with them contrary action and a different mind set. It's like having a new pair of glasses after wearing the wrong prescription for years. You'll begin to see things differently. At first this will be awkward, maybe somewhat overwhelming, but with time, willingness, and faith, as clarity prevails, you'll wonder how and why you ever lived the way you did.

Oh yes, don't forget about *Rule 62*, which is, *"Don't take yourself too seriously."* Remember, there are now, from this point on, no "big deals". That doesn't mean that some of life's occurrences aren't serious and deeply felt. It simply means we shouldn't lose a day's work over a hangnail. The truth is, we have an uncanny ability to blow things up and out of proportion, so take it slow and easy and don't make it more than it really is. If you're not sure as to the relevance of something, get a second opinion. *It's always in your best interest to get a second opinion!*

The reason this process works so well is because it brings forth change, not only in your actions, but also in your attitudes and your thoughts. These attitude and thought adjustments change your values and desires, which in turn lead to a more conducive relationship with your environment and the people in it. All change begins with an honest decision, from within, to be rid of what is, and to accept what can be. The truth is, our progression is held back only by our own perceived limitations. For example, it seemed that every time I went to my father (the man I admire most in the world) as a child, with a thought or idea about a new product or a new method, I would always get the same three responses:

NOTE

"You can't do that!"

"You won't do that!"

"Why don't you leave that to those people who know about that kind of thing?"

Wow! Responses like that took all the wind out of my sails every time, and always left me with more self-doubt, lack of assuredness and loss of self-confidence. Rather than let the negative comments go, my mind always seemed to carry those burdens and resentments everywhere and into all aspects of my life. So, even though I did not plant the original negative thought, it was my mind that always twisted it, and turned it, so that I ended up on the short end (self-sabotage).

The point I'm trying to make is that as long as we stay subservient to ourselves and our situations, thoughts and behaviors, we are <u>under</u> their control, rather than <u>in</u> control of them. However, the moment we decide that we're not going to live like that anymore, wonderful things begin to happen. And they will, if we have a plan of action. (If you don't have a plan, you're not going to know what to do differently. If you don't know what to do, good intentions won't last long and you'll be right back where you started.

This is the plan of action:

We create for you a new heartfelt desire for change. Your change will derive from daily tasks consisting of positive actions that will promote and result in your life changing —

www.bradleyquick.com

www.bradleyquick.com

NOTE

C.L.E.A.N. P.A.C.E. You will have new abilities, new enthusiasm, more hope and positive ambitions for achieving your goals.

I'll bet you're getting pushed around and don't even know it. We've all heard the term, "Getting your buttons pushed." Have you ever thought what that phrase means? It's just like the poor guy out in the field of combat carefully traipsing through the minefields, trying not to step on one and lose life or limb. Are you surrounded by fearful people like that? Your friends and family, more times than not, must delicately maneuver themselves through interactions with you. They are unsure as to what to say or how to say it, what to do or how to do it. Are they wondering if you're going to explode or not?

If, on occasion you have a tendency to over-react with rage, or anger, and generally have a very short fuse in response to those around you, you're probably getting your buttons pushed. This simply means that all the past experiences that you brushed aside and/or buried through your substance(s) and/or behaviors are still just under the surface of your skin and can be activated by the very smallest applied pressure. You're not just subject to what is current, you're also subject to all that was and has been for you in your past. Scary, isn't it? Just think, you're still carrying all that baggage with you wherever you go, to every situation you're in, and whomever your dealing with is subject to it.

The important thing is, at this point, not to allow yourself to add to those existing kegs of emotion that are so near the surface and ready to explode. By following the simple daily tasks as outlined in this Chapter, you can at least stop adding to your arsenal of explosive emotions. If you'll thoroughly read about *Resentments* in the *Glossary* or *Daily Journal* sections, it will show you how to uncover, discover and discard all of your past issues so that you no longer are forced to carry those issues with you and into your present daily life experiences. Take your time! However, when you're ready, this task will optimize your hard drive. Smile…

Checklist

1. First things first. Ask yourself: Am I happy, sad, excited, depressed, or angry? Am I wallowing in hate, ecstatically in love, or in terrible fear? Do I feel lonely, separate, different or afraid? You must first determine your current state of mind then make a self-assessment.

For example: Ask yourself, "How do I feel?" Your answer may be: "I'm hungry, angry, lonely and tired. So, I'm going to (H.A.L.T.) stop, take a deep breath and realize it's time to take care of myself. I'm going to eat something, go to some quiet place (even in my car), and take a short power nap." *I will revitalize myself and start again with a new perspective.*

2. Easy does it. Go to the *Glossary* section of this book and find the most accurate term describing your current feelings and emotions. Read and understand the definition(s). Take a deep breath and read it again. Fully understand the feeling or emotion (cause and effect) before taking action.

3. Acceptance. Now accept what is! Life is what it is at this moment and it can be nothing but what it is right now (snap your fingers and say, *"Just Right Now!"*) Try to stay in this moment. Not in a moment that has yet to be, nor the moment that will never be again. Stay here, right here, right

www.bradleyquick.com

www.bradleyquick.com

<u>NOTE</u>

now. Look down, find your feet and realize there is only this moment and this is where you are. You're just fine, and you'll be just fine no matter what your head says. F.A.S.T. (Faith, Acceptance, Service, This Too Shall Pass)

4. Implementation. P.A.C.E. (Positive Action Cures Everything) Ask yourself: What action will benefit this moment the most? What action will benefit those involved in this situation the most? Is this action based on self (my perceived wants, needs or desires), or is this action I'm about to take based on the needs of others? What would the person whom I respect the most do in this circumstance?

Understanding: To truly understand your own motives, is to truly comprehend the situation and to offer an unselfish response.

Affirmations for Positive Change *(Training Wheels)*

Allow this to be a daily activity, allow this to change your attitude about yourself, those around you, and the world you're in. Read these aloud, word for word, two or three times a day, and you will experience positive transformation in your life. *Just do it, because it only works if you work it!*

1. I am open to all possibilities before me and know that only good can result from my changing.
2. I respect myself now, which gives me courage to further change and grow.
3. I now accept my past and see how it has shaped my life today.

4. I now accept good in my life and welcome it when it comes.

5. I now trust a higher guidance to lead me in the direction of where I need to be.

6. Today I embrace change and accept it as a necessary part of my growth and expansion.

7. Today I allow myself to prosper by experiencing completion in all my affairs.

8. Today I accept myself as I am and know that only good can result from my changing.

9. Today I have the behavior resources to handle whatever happens in my life without having to resort to substance(s) or disorders to contend with my feelings and emotions.

10. Today I make loving choices for myself and accept good into my life.

11. Today I am committed to taking positive actions that will move me and my projects along.

12. Today I forgive those who hurt me, because they are in pain.

13. Today I accept the guidance from my heart and handle my affairs with honesty.

14. Today I appreciate that change happens in small ways and I will take a small step today toward happiness, prosperity, success and freedom from substance abuse and behavioral disorders.

15. Today I am compassionate and loving to myself in every way.

16. Today I let go of my perfectionism so that I can participate more in the excitement of life.

17. Today I allow the excitement of change to fill my life.

NOTE

www.bradleyquick.com

www.bradleyquick.com

NOTE

18. Today I see beyond my fear and live in the expectancy of leading a joyous, prosperous, substance and disorder free life.

19. Today I release the fear that keeps me from moving on.

20. Today I respect the power of words in creating my reality.

21. Today I am responsible for taking good care of myself.

22. Today, on a continuous basis, I let go of all resentments that keep me away from my greater good.

23. Today I open my heart to the abundance around me.

24. Today I have the ability to say "no" when it's appropriate.   "NO!"

25. Today I acknowledge my fear but go beyond it.

26. Today I let go of painful experiences and understand what purpose they serve in my growth process.

27. Today I walk through each of my fears by taking action towards achieving each of my goals.

28. Today being free from substance abuse and behavioral disorders, I have enough time to take care of what I need to do.

29. Today I am and shall remain free from substance abuse and behavioral disorders, no matter what.

30. Today I have the ability to accept the things I cannot change, the courage to change the things that I can, and I have the wisdom to know the difference.

31. Today I will relax and trust that the good I need will find me, either through my leadership, or the leadership of others.

If this seems a little much for you, don't feel bad. Rome wasn't built in a day. Rome was, however, finally built and still stands today as one of the most popular attractions in the world. I'm not for a moment suggesting that you'll end up being a popular tourist attraction. However, you may end up, through this process, being attractive to those you know and love, someone they like to be around.

If you perceive this to be too much, simply start out with four or five affirmations twice a day, continue those for twenty-one days, and let the change begin. Then choose four or five different ones and repeat the process. Remember the Tortoise and the Hare? *Just carry on daily at a steady* P.A.C.E.

Your Daily Journal

Writing will benefit you in so many ways aside from just keeping you up to date about yourself and where you are on a daily basis. It will allow you the freedom of immediate relief, as your mind processes all that you put on paper. Putting pen to paper is magic, magic that you should take advantage of. All that you must do is to be honest in writing about your current issues, ideas, thoughts, resentments, fears, etc. You may often be able to address your own issues just by writing about them, in your own words, on a daily basis. You will achieve better results with daily efforts in regards to this task.

Once you have put these items on paper, if the relief is not yet yours, take a moment and share what you've written with someone. Just through this sort of thinking out loud sharing process, the freedom will be yours as you broaden your understanding of the subject matter, namely yourself.

www.bradleyquick.com

www.bradleyquick.com

NOTE

If you must, call the Hotline (1.800.329.0474) at that moment. Someone is always there to lend an ear, or a voice in regards to your development. We want you to succeed.

The following is an exercise that I have found to be a life saver. My suggestion is that you make this part of your *Daily Journal* activity. It involves resentments. (*Resentment:* A thought continuously resent through the mind.) Resentments are commonly referred to as the number one offender for people like us because most of us are unable to let go of a resentment. However, there is a method for relief if you're willing to do what it takes. Use the following process and you will achieve freedom from resentments. It sure beats letting someone else live rent free between your ears!

1. In your journal, simply write the name of the person, place, or thing for which you hold the resentment. Then:

2. List the cause of the resentment and a brief explanation. Be precise and to the point. Then:

3. List the ways this affected you. Did it affect your self-esteem, ambitions, or personal relationships? Or was it your pride, pocketbook, personal security or sex relations that were affected? Only you can be the honest judge. However, if in doubt, you may want to call the Hotline, your mentor, or go into the chat room for some assistance from others.

4. You must then list your part in this endeavor. (Yes, you had a part in this.) Were you selfish, self-centered, self-seeking, dishonest, or afraid? Put aside for a moment the anger you're feeling towards the resented party. List your part. Just take a deep breath and do it!

Example:
a. **Name:** Tom.
b. **Cause:** Got the promotion at work that I deserved.
c. **Affects:** My self-esteem, personal relations, ambitions, fear, and pocketbook.
d. **My Part:** I was *selfish* in thinking I should get the position. He's been with the company longer. I was really *dishonest* with my hours on the time card, and he generally works harder than I do. I was *afraid (in fear)* of looking bad to my coworkers, which affects my self-esteem.

After listing these items on paper, using this format, simply call the Hotline or your mentor, read them aloud, then throw them away. This action can free you of these resentments, and you can move on. It works if you work it.

In the future, when the time is right for you, this process can also be used to rid yourself of those grudges (resentments) you've been carrying around with you since your beginning. We all have them. You may not believe it, but they still do have a profound impact on you today. All those people who have upset you, all those things that still make you feel bad or angry, and all those things that you should, or could, have done differently. They all produce grudges or resentments. When the timing is right, simply make a list of names, of all those you harbor resentments towards, and follow the example above and you can be free. It's a wonderful sensation, a newfound freedom. A freedom that you can and must put forth every effort to attain.

I hope that you will take the time to experience this process in full by writing in your *Daily Journal*. The rewards are tremendous, and the growth will be substantial. We have provided, at the back of this book, a few pages to get you started

NOTE

www.bradleyquick.com

www.bradleyquick.com

NOTE

on your daily writings. Go to the store and get a spiral binder to keep all your writings in one place. You will also need a highlighter to mark portions of this handbook. Who knows, one day you might have enough positive experiences to put together your own self discovery recovery handbook. Good luck!

Avoidance

Our mind's ability to engage in complete avoidance is much like being in a subconscious state. We've all been there. In that state, we do everything we can and everything that's needed to continue our using and/or abusing. We do anything and everything to get our substance(s) and continue to participate in our disorders. We do whatever it takes to acquire that fix. While in that *acquisition state,* we know nothing else, we see nothing else, and we seem to overcome and avoid everything in our path that might obstruct us from our goal: the next fix.

This is the very reason why smoking is so very appealing to most of us throughout our lives. Cigarettes, cigars and chewing tobacco provide us with a complete, legal, socially accepted, narcotic-enhanced fix. They provide us with the ability to lessen the impact of, and escape from, experiencing the full magnitude of our feelings, all the time and every time. Nicotine affects your brain much the same way as heroin and alcohol. That's why the American Medical Association (AMA) has now classified nicotine as a narcotic. That's why so many of us find it easier to stop other forms of substances, yet continue to smoke. Smoking lessens the impact of life, and allows us to avoid the impact of the newness of life without abuse, yet still provides us with a constant narcotic stream, the mind altering substance nicotine.

I smoked for seventeen years, including my first year of freedom from using and abusing. I then found it to be more detrimental to my coping abilities and health to continue to ingest this narcotic nicotine than it was to learn to live life without it. A big transition, but well worth it!

On the other side of that decision, I have a friend that has been free for more years than me from his substances of choice, alcohol and drugs. Yet he still smokes. He says that he's not willing to start over again, that he doesn't want to be "new" again if it means giving up his nicotine fix. I asked him what he meant by that (wanting to hear it from him). He replied, "I would have to learn to cope with feelings and emotions all over again as if I was brand new at this, and I'm not willing to do that, to start again."

Remember, earlier I addressed the issue of getting caught in that downward spiral. The more you try to break free, the more it pulls you in, and the tougher it is to escape. The secret is to get out as soon as you can. The sooner the better, and the easier it is to set yourself free. F.A.S.T. Rely on this process and you will experience freedom from substance abuse and behavioral disorders.

I Am What I Eat

If you eat junk, expect to feel like junk. If you eat well, expect to feel well. It's that simple. Not really magic at all. You are what you eat. The definition of diet is "method of eating". That's it. You've probably explored different methods of eating your whole life. A lot, a little, healthy and not so healthy, no fats, all carbohydrates, no red meat, five meals a day, one meal a day. I know, I've tried them all.

Let us not forget the real pleasure and how wonderful it feels to eat our favorite foods or rather,

NOTE

www.bradleyquick.com

99

www.bradleyquick.com

NOTE

in some cases, to mask our feelings and emotions by devouring our favorite foods. The only time such eating feels bad for me is when I'm done. I can still hear that commercial, "I can't believe I ate the whole thing," and see that obscenely obese man in gastric pain again. My suggestion is to stay away from all those preservatives, additives and fast foods, those partially dehydrogenated oils and garbage being thrown at us by corporate America's food giants. There is a lot of trash out there being offered to us through the media and specialized advertising that we're expected to gobble up without protest.

The USDA has established its recommended daily allowance (RDA) of vitamins supposedly needed to sustain a healthy body. Some say the only problem is that the recommended amount is only about 2% of what you really need to sustain a healthy body and mind. However, this RDA is the basic standard of the American convenience food diet. Some literature says we need as much as 500 times the vitamins than could possibly be consumed in one day. There is a lot of room for variation between 2% and 500 times what we could eat in one day. What I'm suggesting is that you take a serious look at what you're eating (or what's eating you), why you're eating it, and the benefits of how an adjustment in your diet may bring forth positive change for your body and mind.

My suggestion is that, from this point onward, you eat only fresh and whole foods, take vitamin supplements daily, and drink at least 8 to 10 large glasses of water per day. Come on, this won't kill you. In fact, you will feel so much better as a result. There are even a few fast food chains that offer foods fresh, not frozen, and not full of preservatives. Do your research.

The bottom line is this: the more nutritious food you consume, while drinking a more than adequate amount of water (see *Change Your Water,*

Change Your Life in Resources section), the better you'll feel and the longer you'll last. Then there's the fact that some of us may be also hypoglycemic, allergic to sugar (everyone is sensitive to sugar to some extent) and/or diabetic. Think about it. After all the ways we've abused our bodies, we now deserve to take care of our physical selves. Do yourself a favor and get your body checked out. Schedule a complete physical, with a blood test for cholesterol, and a check of your blood pressure. You'll be glad you did and you will know where you stand as you start this new way of living.

On a daily basis, I like to consume:

Vitamin A & D 400 to 600 IU.

Vitamin B100 100 mg.

Vitamin C 3000 to 5000 mg (1000 mg3 to 5 times daily).

Vitamin E 400 to 800 IU.

Zinc 100 mg.

My typical daily diet consists of the following:

Fresh fruit in the morning.

Salad and/or chicken at lunch.

Dinner that includes no or few carbohydrates or starches.

Nonfat frozen yogurt snack at night.

This method of eating seems to work for me. If I eat carbohydrates, I wear them. If I eat grease, I wear it. If I don't eat foods conducive to my body's needs, without going overboard too often, I suffer the consequences. The right diet, combined with enough sleep and daily exercise is my answer to maintaining, not only a level frame of mind, but also a body that feels and looks good.

Just think how very complex the human body really is. Man cannot duplicate this body of ours. Yet with every opportunity he gets, man tries to put some new additive (food) in it because it tastes good or makes the food last longer. This country spends more per year on diets than any other

NOTE

www.bradleyquick.com

www.bradleyquick.com

NOTE
---

country in the world, yet it's population is among the most obese and physically out of shape in the world.

We cannot change the habits of the world or of this country, we can only change our own habits, in our little world and in our bodies. So make up your mind to feel better, to think better, and to be better. Be the best you can be, through proper nutrition, sleep, and exercise. In addition, I find if I eat late at night, after 8 p.m., I don't sleep very well. As a result of not sleeping well, I end up not having the full and complete day I might have otherwise had. The fact is that downtime, or sleep time, is when your body has an opportunity to rejuvenate, cleanse, and repair itself. It is for that purpose that we sleep, to awaken refreshed and energetic. So when your body must expend 50% of its energy while sleeping to digest that late night meal, you're not getting the full benefit of that sleep time. This results in a bad night's sleep that turns into a day that probably would have been better had you gotten some decent rest. *Be aware of what you are eating and why you're eating it.*

Stop Cravings The Quick Way

Stop Cravings

I believe I have found the expert (Dr, Hyla Cass) with the perfect nutritional formulas to alleviate your cravings and make your journey from dependence to healthy independence more assured. The following knowledge and supplements will make your detoxification and recovery journey much easier and more efficient. I wish I'd had these nutritional supplements in early recovery when I was detoxifying.

Bradley

(The Quick Fix Holistic Formula) Healthy Brain, Healthy Mind, Healthy Purpose

NOTE

by Hyla Cass M.D.

Bradley asked me share my ideas on his treating addiction, compulsion, and obsession nutritionally, a field that I have been involved with as an integrative psychiatrist for over 20 years. On reviewing his manuscript, I was delighted to see how well aware he is of the effects of nutrition on addictions and brain function. He's done a remarkable job of correcting his own brain imbalances with good nutrition, exercise, restorative sleep, positive thinking, and devotion to working life enhancement processes like *The Quick Fix*, which will be explained in this Chapter.

As addictions are progressive, so is recovering from those addictions! I believe that your recovery will progress better if you use specific supplements to restore your brain's chemical balance. Why? There are millions of chemical reactions that occur every second in every cell of your body. These very important reactions require specific nutrients in order to function properly. Particularly sensitive are our *neurons* or nerve cells, requiring just the right raw materials to manufacture our *neurotransmitters* (chemical messengers that control our mind, mood, and behavior). When we don't have the materials we need, we become depressed, drowsy, irritable, or agitated, or we can't think or concentrate properly.

So, along come our fixes, (whatever substances we abuse happen to be): caffeine, sugar, methamphetamine, or perhaps cocaine to "sharpen" our mind and raise our energy level; alcohol, Valium, marijuana or any number of prescribed medications to calm us down; or heroin and nicotine to

www.bradleyquick.com

www.bradleyquick.com

NOTE
---

take us away from it all. The problem is, we're not giving the cells what they really need, and we're just fooling them for a brief moment with harmful substances. Not only does this temporary fix wear off, we're then left feeling much worse than before! We may continue chasing that initial high, hoping in some delusional way that it will return with the next dose, and we become caught in the cycle of addiction.

The good news is that there's a healthy fix (*The Quick Fix Holistic Formula*) that actually works in restoring your maximum brain function with no withdrawal or other bad effects. Since neurotransmitters are literally made from nutrients—amino acids, vitamins, and minerals—we can formulate the perfect "brain food" to restore them, and break the cycle of addiction. Nutritional supplements can restore balance, and create a state of high energy, increased focus, and good mood, with no withdrawal or side effects, since you're giving your brain cells exactly what they need to operate at their best. *The Quick Fix Holistic Formula* works quite quickly and effectively. This is why:

Here are the neurotransmitters and their functions:

- Stimulating: Dopamine, norepinephrine (NE)
- Calming: serotonin, GABA
- Mind and memory: acetylcholine

Sugar Blues

Sugar addiction is closely related to most of the other addictions. By keeping your blood sugar level even throughout the day with the proper diet and supplements, you can avoid those dips that lead to cravings for alcohol or cocaine (or any other unhealthy substance). I also recommend the supplements chromium and glutamine to help reduce sugar cravings.

The Quick Fix Holistic Prescription

Now that we know the relationship between brain chemistry and addiction, let's see what to add to your program to first help stop your downward spiral and then, to restore your brain chemistry balance to an even higher level.

In addition to a multi vitamin-mineral formula, I suggest the following, twice daily unless otherwise noted. I have added in parentheses the product(s) that contains these nutrients:

1. Chromium (200 mcg) and glutamine (500 mg twice daily and also as needed for cravings) to regulate blood sugar and thereby reduce brain fog and cravings for sugar, alcohol, or drugs. (Brain Recovery packets)

2. 5-hydroxytryptophan (5-HTP) 200-400 mg at bedtime both for depression and sleep problems, to boost serotonin levels. (Brain Recovery PM)

3. Calming amino acids, theanine 200 mg and taurine 500 -1000 mg to boost GABA when he was anxious or irritable; calming herbs valerian 100 mg (or 100-200 at bedtime), lemon balm, passion flower (CALM Natural Mind; added valerian in Nightly CALM)

4. Tyrosine (500-1000 mg) or phenylalanine (500-1000 mg) to boost dopamine for enhanced mood and concentration (Brain Recovery AM)

5. Specific brain cell nutrients such as phosphatidyl serine(100 mg) and phosphatidyl choline (GPC 500 mg), acetyl-l-carnitine (500 mg), and ginkgo (60 – 90 mg) to enhance acetylcholine, brain blood flow and brain cell health (Brain Balance)

www.bradleyquick.com

www.bradleyquick.com

NOTE
---

6. "Adaptogenic" herbs such as ashwaganda, and ginseng to restore his burned out adrenal glands, which were burned out by long-term stress (EnergyBalance)

7. Omega 3 fatty acids in the form of fish oil 1000 mg twice daily to help restore the cell wall in which neurotransmitters are made. (Brain Recovery Packets)

8. Extra B vitamins (50-100 mg) and magnesium 200 mg. to handle the depletion due to addiction and stress. They are essential in producing the neurotransmitters. (Brain Recovery)

To order and find more information about *The Quick Fix Holistic Formula,* go to Bradley's website www.bradleyquick.com and look under *The Quick Fix Holistic Formula Supplements* link. Use the Discount Promotional Code "QuickFix."

THE QUICK FIX Holistic Formula – Nutrients for Peak Recovery

To make it simple, I have created a system of specific encapsulated formulas that work together to enhance brain function:

Dr. Cass Brain Recovery AM and PM Packets™: The AM packet is taken with breakfast, the PM packet with dinner.
- A high quality, high potency broad-spectrum multivitamin and mineral formula that provides the essential nutrients and co-factors needed to balance and restore body and brain chemistry.
- Contains nutrients that diminish sugar cravings, encourage fat loss, and aid in

preventing age-related changes, including Alzheimer's disease and dementia.

- A high dose of one of the most potent anti-oxidants and liver support nutrients, alpha lipoic acid, essential for neutralizing free radical damage to the cells and restoring liver function.
- Precursors (5-HTP, tyrosine, glutamine, taurine) and supportive nutrients (B6, inositol) to optimize neurotransmitters.
- Controls cravings and restores brain chemistry in substance abuse recovery.
- Excellent for ADD, anxiety, and depression.
- Essential fatty acids (EPA, DHA) essential for formation of brain cells and neurotransmitters, and is a key nutrient for healing depression, bipolar disorder, ADHD, and addiction. They combat inflammation, improve cardiac function, enhance immunity, and balance hormones.

Dr. Cass' BrainBalance™ Formula:
- Powerful revitalizing nutrients for brain protection and brain blood flow.
- Restore and maintain brain cell function for optimum mood, cognition and memory.
- Some of these nutrients can be felt within several hours (acetyl-L-carnitine, GPC, inositol), and others (phosphatidylserine, ginkgo) over months, as they gradually restore your brain cells.

Dr. Cass' CALM Natural Mind Formula™:
- Safe and effective replacement for drugs and alcohol: Calms your mind and relieves stress — without side effects, impairment, drowsiness, or loss of judgment.
- Restores your brain chemistry (especially GABA) rather than depleting it.

NOTE

www.bradleyquick.com

www.bradleyquick.com

NOTE

- Enhances mood and sharpens mental acuity.

Dr. Cass' Nightly CALM™ – for sleep
- Same as CALM but with added valerian, a proven non-addictive, hangover-free herbal sedative.

Dr. Cass' EnergyBalance Natural Mind Formula™
- Feel-good, energizing neurotransmitters.
- Support the adrenal glands — the core of your energy system — while enhancing energy, improving mood and promoting inner balance.

Dr. Cass' FOCUS Formula™:
- Acts like a cup of coffee, but without the letdown, addictiveness, and other downsides.
- Promotes mental clarity, alertness and a positive mood state without the side effects of herbal or prescription stimulants.
- Perfectly balanced blend of amino acids, vitamins, minerals and antioxidants that produces the two major mood- and atten-tion- enhancing neurotransmitters, norepi-nephrine and dopamine.

To order and find more information about *The Quick Fix Holistic Formula*, go to Bradley's website www.bradleyquick.com and look under *The Quick Fix Holistic Formula Supplements* link. Use the Discount Promotional Code "QuickFix."

I recommend that everyone who is dealing with brain chemistry imbalance begin with **the Brain Recovery AM and PM packets.** If you're experiencing sleep problems, add **Nightly CALM.** For problems with brain function, including memory and clarity of thought, add **BrainBalance. For added alertness and concentration, add FOCUS. For adrenal support and sustained energy, take ENERGY.**

Most people find they do best when they take the whole system, since each component has its unique role. **They all work well together, so there's no need to worry about interactions or taking too much.** You'll find that you can decrease your dose over time, but do stay on a maintenance program to keep your mind sharp, your mood even, and to help prevent cravings that may lead to a relapse.

Since my program is a work-in-progress based on the latest research, don't be surprised if you see additional or modified products when you go to my website.

Recommended usage:

Start with the Brain Recovery AM and PM packets for 2 to 3 weeks so your body can adapt, and you can observe the results. After that, add in the specific 'extras' as needed. After 12 weeks on the full program, you can taper down the extras by 1/3 to 1/2 as a maintenance dose, while taking the packets indefinitely as your daily health booster. As many others have, you may just find the effects to be astonishing!

To order and find more information about *The Quick Fix Holistic Formula,* go to Bradley's website www.bradleyquick.com and look under *The Quick Fix Holistic Formula Supplements* link. Use the Discount Promotional Code "QuickFix."

Eating for Peak Recovery

It's also vitally important to eat well in order to restore and maintain your brain function and remain substance abuse free. Here are the essential basics:

NOTE

www.bradleyquick.com

www.bradleyquick.com

NOTE

- Eat whole foods and fresh foods; avoid processed foods.
- Eat three servings a day of top-quality protein foods—fish, poultry, lean meat (free range), egg, soy, or combinations of beans, lentils, and grains.
- Choose *complex* carbohydrates such as whole grains, vegetables, and most fruits, and avoid sugar and refined foods.
- Eat fish three times a week, or take fish-oil supplements.
- Drink at least a quart of water (Hexagonal Water if possible www.TheQuickFixWater.com), if not two or more, a day, either pure or in diluted juices and herbal or fruit teas.
- Minimize your intake of tea, coffee, and soft drinks.
- Eat lots of antioxidant-rich fruits and vegetables—at least five servings a day.

For details on diet, blood sugar, neurotransmitters, and specific nutrients, read my book Natural Highs (www.cassmd.com).

Common Myths of Addiction

After treating hundreds of substance abusers addicted to substances from alcohol, cocaine, heroin and prescription drugs, to "socially accepted drugs" like caffeine, tobacco and sugar, I have seen how a series of popular myths has often clouded the issue of addiction. Once the correct treatment is given, the "addictive personality" often disappears and one has the opportunity to grow up. This, of course, does not negate the tremendous importance of the social and emotional support groups, psychotherapy, and life enhancement programs like The Quick Fix, but adds the missing piece to treatment and relapse prevention. It also allows you to begin to examine old traumas which themselves cause chronic (and often unconscious) stress, which continues to deplete your brain chemistry.

Here are some popular misconceptions:

Myth #1: Compulsive use of an addictive substance is a sign of weakness or poor moral character.

Fact: You are not a weak or "bad" person. Rather, you have a brain chemistry imbalance, and moral character may have little to do with it. To prove the point, researchers took a group of rats, made them "alcoholic" then treated them with amino acids. When tested further, they had lost their cravings and addiction. Of course, human beings are more complex, have social cues, and emotional baggage—all best dealt with by a well-nourished brain.

Myth #2: Chronic addiction is a disease that can be treated with prescription drugs.

Fact: While you may have a chemical imbalance, it's not likely a Prozac, OxyContin, Xanax, Zoloft, Paxil, or Wellbutrin deficiency. As a psychiatrist who can prescribe drugs but chooses not to, I deplore the standard treatment of medicating those in withdrawal, often heavily and with multiple drug "cocktails." This approach not only taxes an already overloaded system, but does not get to the root cause. It also interferes with mental and emotional rehabilitation. You can't do much in therapy or a life enhancement program when you're in a medication-induced fog.

Myth #3: Drugs and alcohol are the cause of substance abuse.

Fact: While using substances will increase the problem, you'll find that the underlying cause is a brain chemistry imbalance and lack of coping

www.bradleyquick.com

www.bradleyquick.com

NOTE
---

skills. Beneath that may be traumatic memories, resentments, shame, and guilt that need to be processed.

Myth #4: Avoiding relapse is a constant struggle for recovering substance abusers.

Fact: Once you're in balance, any craving to use is simply a sign that you need to correct your nutrition and get into positive action.

Myth #5: Relapse is part of recovery:

Fact: Relapse is just a sign of not fully embracing the solution

Myth #6: "Substance abuse runs in my family so I can't help it."

Fact: If you have a family history of substance abuse, you simply have to be more careful than most to take the appropriate nutrients. You are not a slave to your genes!

Hyla Cass, MD is a nationally acclaimed innovator and expert in the field of integrative medicine, psychiatry, and addiction recovery. She is often seen as an expert guest on national radio and television, and quoted in national print media. Dr. Cass is a past Assistant Clinical Professor of Psychiatry at UCLA School of Medicine and author of several popular books including *Natural Highs: Supplements, Nutrition and Mind-Body Techniques, 8 Weeks to Vibrant Health: A Woman's Take-Charge Program*, and *Supplement Your Prescription* (late 2007). (www. cassmd.com)

To order and find more information about *The Quick Fix Holistic Formula*, go to Bradley's website www.bradleyquick.com and look under *The Quick Fix Holistic Formula Supplements* link. Use the Discount Promotional Code "QuickFix."

Stretching

I find it so very important to my well-being, both mentally and physically, to stretch, both before and after exercise, even on day's of relaxation. It loosens me up, allows my circulation to increase, and saves me from cramps, pulled muscles, and the like. It allows my body to move freer, stand taller, and be more limber.

The intent, aside from the above, is to elongate your major muscles, and give them full elasticity. To do that, you must hold the stretch for a count of 12 to 20. That's not a bounce, that's not a half measure, that's a full stretch held for the appropriate count. You will only benefit from doing this. You will feel better, move better, and even have better posture. So as you don't get carried away, I have included my most effective stretches just as they were taught to me.

Remember, muscles have memory. So in stretching, or opening those shut down muscles, you may be subject to feelings and emotions of which you're not sure. This is a normal response by the body, and you will not only survive, but you will be better for it. Drink lots of water, and don't forget to breathe through the stretches

Lower Torso
1st stretch:

Find a raised surface, such as a stair, a curb, etc., and stand with your feet together with your heels hanging over the edge of the surface (always hold onto something for stabilization). Now raise one foot off the ground and lean on the heel still hanging over the raised surface (the stretch should be felt in the calf). Hold this for a count of at least 20 then transfer stance to your other leg.

2nd stretch:

Stand straight, knees together, lifting your heel up behind you to your butt. Hold the heel firm

<u>NOTE</u>

www.bradleyquick.com

www.bradleyquick.com

NOTE

---

for a count of no less than 20, then lift your other heel. This stretch should be felt in the thigh.

3rd stretch:

While standing, lift your leg up (fully extended), and rest your heel on an elevated surface (counter, chair, table) and lean forward. Hold this for a count of no less than 20, and then change legs.

Upper Torso
4th stretch:

While standing straight, extend your arm fully, placing your wrist against a firm object (door jam, light pole, tree), then turn you body in the opposite direction of the arm being extended. Hold this stretch for a count of 20, then switch arms. Feel this stretch in your arm and in your chest.

5th stretch:

Stand straight up, facing the wall. Then take one big step backwards and separate your feet. With feet separated beyond shoulders, extend your arms and lean towards the wall, resting your palms on the wall. In this position, extend your face and chest down towards the floor for a count of no less than 20. Feel this stretch in your arms and shoulders.

CHAPTER 11

Life, It's a Universal Thing

Which has been around longer, you or the Universe? The Universe and all of its properties, living and otherwise, has been around for millions of years. On the other hand, comparatively speaking, we've been here for about 10 seconds. Yet, I've found myself, over and over, dictating just how the world and all of its inhabitants should act, think, behave and most of all how they should treat me. My perception has been, sometimes more than others, sure that I'm the most important thing in, and the center of, the Universe (total self obsession). Think about it. How many times, in your eyes, has it been all about you? There's more to this world than just you and I. There really is!

Let's take a moment and talk about our planet. Because of the perfect gravitational pull on the face of this beautiful planet earth we can walk, stand, get up or sit down at our own leisure without much effort. If this gravitational pull was any greater than it is, our faces would be stuck to the ground. On the other hand, if gravitation was any weaker than it is, we, along with everything else on the planet would be floating around. Neither any more, nor any less gravity would be conducive to life as we know it. It's perfect just the way it is.

This planet is also tilted to one side on a 23.45 degree axis. Because of that fact alone we are subject to the four seasons, winter, spring, summer and fall. So because this planet is spinning around at approximately 1,000 mph we have perfect gravity and because we are on a 23.45 degree tilt we get the four seasons. Perfect so far, isn't it? Wait, it gets better!

www.bradleyquick.com

www.bradleyquick.com

NOTE

While this beautiful planet of ours is spinning around at 1,000 mph on a 23.45 degree axis, it's also orbiting around the sun at 67,000 mph. And the fact is, that if during this 67,000 mph orbit around the sun this planet were to sway one inch further away from the sun than it does we would freeze. It would be much too cold to sustain life as we know it. On the same note, if this beautiful planet of ours were to sway one inch closer to the sun than it does at its closest point to the sun, we would burn up. It would be much too hot to support life as we know it. You get the idea? It's just perfect.

Let's now think about the strange things that happen on our planet, All those green living things we take for granted, (trees, bushes, plants) breath in almost everything that we, and every other living creature on the face of the planet, exhales (carbon dioxide). At the same time almost everything that is generated by all this green life (oxygen) is inhaled by every living, breathing creature on the face of the planet. Oxygen is what keeps us alive and technically it's a poisonous gas (kind of odd). Which way do the geese fly in the winter time? That's right, south! Bet they didn't fly by your place asking for directions. How about the caterpillar that builds a cocoon and emerges as a butterfly? What about the salmon that hatches in a creek up in the mountains and then makes its way down through rivers and streams to the ocean (a small body of water covering two thirds the face of the planet). They just swim around there until their internal alarm goes off which sends them back up through the rivers, against the currents, to where they came from in order to spawn. And what animal is sitting in the waters waiting for those fish? The mighty bear (who just happens to love salmon)!. Think about it... the squirrel and the acorn, the bird and the worm, the bee and the honey, the fish and the bear... nature's wonders and it all works just perfectly...without our help.

Now, let's talk about the human body. The same one that we often have a tendency to take for granted and abuse (remember, it's the only one you've got). The human body is a spectacular machine. Do you know that every cell, molecule, atom and chromosome in your body knows exactly what it's supposed to do? Each of those hundreds of billions of components that make up your body, don't have to ask for directions, go to school, or study in order to work in perfect harmony with each other. They just do!

Every one of us has unique identifying factors. Each of our fingerprints are totally unique, one of a kind. All of us have individual DNA, again differentiating each of us as individuals. We are all one of a kind, with many similarities but each of us is still unique and individual.

Which brings me to this point. If every living thing on the face of this planet, microorganism to elephant, inherently knows what it's doing and instinctually has a path for its existence, where do we fit in? What is the difference between all these living things and us? How come they all know what they're doing and we've always had a rough time figuring that out? I believe the reason is that we have the ability to choose and they don't. Not all our decisions are based solely upon the instinctual basics. We possess the ability to make up our own minds as to which way we're going, what we're doing, what we're saying and what we're going to do to deal with our feelings and emotions. The only issue with that is that I've always been an immediate gratification junkie. I don't know about you but my solution was to find a quick way to fix me and fix me now! Especially when I was confronted with feelings and emotions that I did not know how or wish to contend with. The obsessive compulsive disorder that I'm suffering from

www.bradleyquick.com

www.bradleyquick.com

NOTE

always won out over my instincts, every time! It won out over my best interest, my best intentions and my best true desires.

The solution is to become willing to change and to do all that you must do in order to find your role and purpose in the evolution of this planet. Every living thing, you included, has an individual roll in this evolutionary process of life. Just because we're the most selfish, self-destructive, hedonistic, emotionally driven animals on this planet doesn't mean that we don't each have a real individual purpose here other than just procreation. The ability to find your purpose is regulated only by you and your willingness to change. You can change if you work this process and to listen to your inner voice, the true self, and learn to act on your instincts (first thought to mind) not on your fears or self-seeking desires.

So here's the challenge: You must become willing to uncover, discover and discard the past. Become willing to work this process daily and to humbly open yourself up to the sunlight of the spirit (the powers that be in this universe) so that you can be inspired intuitively with a thought or decision that's in accordance with the will of the universe for you and your life. Once you do find your purpose you will discover, while participating in (positive action) your purpose, that you have never been so high, felt so free, felt so fulfilled and possibly never experienced so much love in your life. You will find that you have become the best you that has ever existed. You will find that your reality often times shadows those dreams that you thought would never be.

Remember, the universe and all its inhabitance have been around for millions of years while you and I have been here for about 10 seconds. Let's jump in and become an active member in the perfectness of what is and what can be for all of us. Practicing these principals and putting forth the right efforts, with these ideals in mind, you will become happy, joyous and free.

www.bradleyquick.com

NOTE

A

Abandonment:

Feeling deserted and left alone. We have all suffered this to some extent, and rational or not, it seems to be a very hopeless state. This feeling, or condition, can have a large impact on our current and future actions. Our social interactions will be enhanced or diminished by our mind's willingness to cope with this issue. It is what it is, and it was what it was. And it can only be what we are willing to accept without the fear of abandonment.

Acceptance:

Understanding that things happen over which we have no control. Acceptance is the common denominator among all our problems today. When we are disturbed, it is because we find some person, place, thing or situation, some fact of our lives, unacceptable to us. We can find no peace until we accept that person, place, thing, or situation as being exactly the way it is at this moment. Until we could accept life on life's terms, we could not be happy. Until we could accept our substance abuse issues, we could not move on and be free. We need to concentrate not so much on what needs to be changed in the world and in its attitudes, as on what needs to be changed in ourselves and in our attitudes. We must also not forget that we were born perfect, just as we should be, a product of nature, flawless in many ways, a perfect part of this universe. It wasn't until our best thinking, coupled with our situational outcomes, began to get us in trouble that self-doubt set in, leaving us hopeless, helpless and feeling different from the rest. Accepting ourselves, as we are at this moment, is essential to our individual well-being. Accepting that today is the first day of the rest of our lives is essential to starting a new existence.

Achievement:

Reaching a goal. Success, or achievement, even in small degrees, can be as hard to cope with as failure. They both require coping mechanisms. Now that you're achieving success by committing to the principals in this handbook, remember that you deserve it. Now go help somebody and strive to achieve more, and remember: Easy does it!

Affirmation:

A positive declaration for change voiced by an individual repetitively throughout a given time period for a definite purpose. Read your declaration of change aloud, and you'll begin to believe that which you are reading. Believe them, and you will change your self-image for the better and only good will come of it. The better you are to yourself, the better you are to the world.

Amends:

To improve one's conduct and hence, to remove faults. We rectify abuses, mistakes, correct errors, and reform or amend our lives. Confession and truth as to our part in any and all matters brings us freedom. Therefore, we do not hesitate for a moment to admit when we are wrong and apologize for any harm done. We do this on the spot. We do this so as not to carry all the negative feelings and emotions with us into our future

Anger:

A severe feeling of dis-ease or fear. We avoid retaliation and argument. Take a deep breath and realize that people are just doing their perceived best to get through this moment in life — right, wrong or indifferent. We have also caused much anger for many people throughout our lives. Therefore, show them the same tolerance, pity, and patience that you would expect to be shown by a friend. Remember, anger is generally associated with fear, of either losing something we've got or not getting something we want. Maybe your anger is resulting from a bruised ego. It's so easy to get angry when someone, through their actions or words, makes us look bad. That verifies our lack of self-esteem. You look like you look, and you are who you are. As long as your intentions are admirable, don't let your ego get in the way. Tolerance and understanding is our code. P.A.C.E.

Annoyance:

To irritate or bother, as by a repeated action. I used to be an annoyance to the world and those around me. My family and friends suffered the most. Now my family and friends benefit from my existence. Don't be an annoyance. P.A.C.E.

Anticipation:

Waiting for something to happen. The only tools I possess to evaluate my anticipation are my past experiences, and for the most part I want nothing to do with my past. So whether I hope for, look forward to, wait for, or count on something, I lose. I must stay in the moment, for that is all I can be sure of, what is here and now.

Assume:

Makes an *ASS of U and ME.* Assumptions are dangerous, particularly when your mind is clouded by your experiences with substance abuse and behavioral disorders. Drawing a conclusion and/or relying on expectations falls into the ASSUME category.

B

Bottom:

Usually referred to as *Hitting The Bottom.* The moment you realize that your actions, beliefs, and motives change for the worse is the very moment you are at your bottom, and you can only go up from there. To hit the bottom, just quit digging.

Buttons:

Pushing my buttons. The truth is, when we are irritated it is usually not just by what is happening now but also by our past experiences. Our past has a tendency to color our relationship to what is going on today. Therefore, you are not just subject to what is, you're also subject, in the now, to all that was and has been your experience, forever. (*Resentment:* A thought continuously resent through the mind).

C

Change:
To make things different, to alter one's life for the better brings forth positive change. However, change generally brings with it fear. We call it fear of the unknown. The easiest way for me to experience change is to stay in the moment. And do the job that's put in front of me to the best of my ability and stay out of the results. Remember, we are in the efforts business, not the results business. If we keep doing what we're doing, we'll keep getting what we're getting. If we want something different we must do something different. No change, no gain!

Character Defects:
Traits in our personality that we would be better off without. Our goal is to eliminate character defects. Jump into this process, let's change!

C.L.E.A.N:
Clearly Learning Everything Absolutely Necessary today to achieve our goal of being free from substance abuse and disorders of all kinds. Knowledge is power. It's time to energize by just doing what it takes today, in this moment, to practice and learn this process, *The Quick Fix.*

Control (fear):
Being in charge of what happens. By relinquishing control, we embrace the world. By hanging on to supposed control, we remain in fear of the unknown. We can only win and enjoy true freedom by letting go of control and having faith in ourselves and the universe that we can meet the challenges of the unknown.

Coping Mechanism:
The mind's natural ability to deal or cope with perceived stimuli. Once I started to buffer my feelings and emotions with substances and/or dysfunctional behaviors, I no longer needed to rely on my natural abilities to cope or to deal with my feelings and emotions. Happy, sad, excited, depressed or angry, in hate, in love or in fear, I always resorted to substances and dysfunctional behaviors in order to cope. When you stop

www.bradleyquick.com

fixing yourself with substances or behaviors, you must learn to cope without them. That's when your natural and true coping mechanisms begin to be nurtured through experience. Your natural coping abilities ceased to mature the moment you started using and abusing on a consecutive basis. Substances, and/or dysfunctional behaviors became your solution. Take away that solution, substances and behaviors, and you're left with the problem. You and your inability to deal with feelings and emotions, life on life's terms, has now evolved into an issue for you. So it is now time to fill that void with this *Quick Fix Process* which will allow you to grow up and mature just as nature had planned for you to do.

D

Depression:
Fear of losing what you have or not getting what you want. Low spirits, unhappiness, gloom, dejection, misery, trouble, worry, hopelessness, distress, desperation. This emotion will infect us all at one time or another, guaranteed. All that we can do is write about it, share it with somebody, and try our best to help others. Be confident that this discomfort, over time, will pass. Remember, if you can get out of yourself by being of service to someone else, even if just for a moment, it's to your benefit, especially in this time of inner turmoil. Reach out and help someone. You'll feel better, you really will.

Dishonesty:
Lying, cheating, and stealing are common examples of dishonesty. Dishonesty brings with it arrogance, treachery, crookedness, corruption, backbiting and double-crossing, and is a really dishonorable quality. Why would you want to get caught up in such abysmal qualities as this? Be as honest as you can just in this moment, and remember honesty begins with being honest with yourself. This is your choice, and your choice only. Make the choice that best suits you and make it honestly.

E

E.G.O.:

Edging Good Out. Conceit, vanity, false pride, and arrogance are just some of the mindsets that go with being stuck in one's ego. By staying in our ego, we are too concerned and absorbed with self to be aware of all there is to be had, and to be done, in this world. Today I want nothing to do with the thinking that goes along with those types of attitudes. Remember that ego, self-manifested in various ways, is the root of all our problems today. Why would you want to go hang out with a stuck up, pompous, puffed up, self-centered, cocky, overbearing, overconfident person? Get out of the fallacy of self, and you'll be a better person for it.

Emotions:

Any specific feeling; any of various complex reactions with both mental and physical manifestations, reaction to various perceived stimuli. Ask yourself, is my reaction out of fear of loss, or consequence? Pain or pleasure? Is my immediate response one of self-preservation, self-pity, deceit or dishonesty, guilt or shame? You'll have to answer these questions for yourself, examine your motives and "to thine own self be true."

Envy:

To feel ill will toward, have hard feelings toward, and/or to feel resentful toward someone for their perceived advantages. Envy means not being sure who or what we are. Being discontent and having ill will about someone else's perceived advantages and/or possessions is a waste of time and usually based on unreality. None of these feelings are conducive to well-being. I must look at who I am and what I have, as compared to who I was and where I came from. At that point, I can begin to get a new and proper perspective. One solution for avoiding envy is to go help someone less fortunate than yourself. You might share with them your experience as to how you got through what they are currently experiencing. That alone will work wonders. You may also want to refer back to *Acceptance* in this Chapter.

Expectation:
A projected outcome calculated only by our past experience and/or our projected wants, needs, or desires. Stay out of expectations. After all, what will be will be. Stay in the now. Expectation is simply a premeditated resentment.

Exercise:
Physical workout. Exercise is essential to establishing and maintaining clarity, both mental and physical. All that I need to do to change my perception, for the better at any time, is to break a sweat. It doesn't matter if I break a sweat running, swimming, walking, lifting weights, or from any other form of physical exertion. I always benefit by breaking a sweat, as will you. Consult your doctor first so as not to hurt yourself. (I had to say that so as to protect myself. Now go walk around the block.)

F

Faith:
Belief in something we cannot physically see. We must have faith in something other than ourselves. It may be faith in this process, faith in the earth's gravitational pull, or just the faith that tomorrow the sun will rise again followed by the moon. Whatever it is we believe in, we must have faith in something other than ourselves. You may wish to start by just having faith that you can and will work this *Quick Fix Process* and that it can and will work for us.

F.A.S.T.:
Faith, Acceptance, Service, This Too Shall Pass. This is a major key in overcoming and getting through that which comes up for you on your path of life. I have found that I must have faith in something other than myself and my abuses, I must have faith in the process, faith in the universe, faith in others, faith in Mother Nature. Faith must be followed by acceptance. I must accept people, places, things and situations as they are at any given moment, not just as I wish them to be but as they really are at this moment. I must accept me as I am at this moment,

not how I was, not how I will be, but just as I am. I must accept all that is including me so that I may move on.

I must also recognize how I can be of service to others and take the appropriate actions. That will serve two purposes. First, it will allow me to help someone, and through that very action of focusing on another and being of service to them, it will allow me to forget about me for that moment, and that is a very good thing. I feel honored in just having the privilege to help another individual. That includes small gestures as well as large, such as opening the door for someone, making someone smile, doing someone a favor, participating in a task or sometimes just listening to another's problems. You will feel better as a result. Lastly, you must remember this too will pass. It always does, and it always will. It's not 1980 any longer, nor is it last Tuesday. Before you realize, it will be tomorrow, and that will pass as well.

Facade:

A facade is the image of ourselves that we wish the world and all those around us to see. This façade is seldom our real self. Each of us has built a facade. We are really much internally different from the facade we create. This facade usually, at some point in the past, has been consciously or subconsciously created by each of us so that we might be as we perceive the world and its people think we should be (self-preservation). Keep working this process and, bit by bit, your false perception of self will chip away. As it does, your facade will change, and your true self will emerge. I promise.

Fatigue:

Exhaustion; Weariness; Tiredness; a full plate; mounting issues. All of these eruptions of fatigue, and many more, equate to distorted perception and extreme vulnerability. We must slow down and take care of ourselves. Take a nap when one is needed even if only a short one. Continue your regime of healthy food and vitamins!

www.bradleyquick.com

F.E.A.R.:

False Evidence Appearing Real. Fear oftentimes looks so very authentic and true, when behind it all it is nothing but our mind's fabrication of misperceived information. You've heard FDR's famous admonition, "There's nothing to fear but fear itself." It remains true today. Remember, do what you fear most and you control fear. Submitting to fear only brings reckless abandon of the truth. It always helps my clarity when I allow someone other than myself to provide his or her opinion about what I perceive to be fearful. It helps to get another perspective, another interpretation. How deceived I was to think that what I feared most was in the world, instead of what was in my mind.

Feelings:

Emotional reaction to outside stimuli. Feelings are facts, not truths. The fact is, you feel the way you feel even though your feelings may be very far from the truth of the matter. Feelings cannot always be trusted even though we perceive our feelings as reality. The reality we feel between our ears should not be confused with the truth of the situation.

Forgiveness:

Letting go of anger, releasing with love all that we perceive that we have done wrong to ourselves and others. In order to forgive others, we must first forgive ourselves. With that in mind and in heart, we can begin to accept others as they are as we begin to forgive them for not living up to our expectations, or treating us as we think we should be treated. With forgiveness, we can begin to let others live their lives as the fallible human beings they are, going down whatever path they may. Then when they cross our path, we must greet and assist them and forgive them for their errors. After all, we would hope for the same treatment from them.

G

Goal:
Something you hope to achieve, something to strive for, an ambition. By setting a goal, you create a purpose in your life. Having a purpose gives your life meaning and lessens the difficulty of daily living. Without a goal, you're subject to only what life throws at you, your whole life becomes consumed only with contending with that. Having a goal makes all the trials and tribulations of this daily existence seem trivial, especially when your striving for a desired outcome. Set a goal, have a purpose, help others.

Greed:
Selfishness, tight, not giving, wanting everything. Be careful of falling into a pattern of greed, and remember: You can only keep what you have by giving it away.

H

H.A.L.T.
Hungry, Angry, Lonely, Tired. Being subject to these conditions tends to distort your perceived reality, sometimes to the extreme. If at all possible, when these feelings come upon you, it's best to HALT, stop and fill the void, by napping, eating, calling someone, putting it on paper, etc. Positive action will generally correct your condition and reestablish your equilibrium.

Honesty:
Telling the truth. If you're anything like me, that's always been difficult. More often than not (even when reporting what I thought to be the truth), it was always based on my perception, my fear, my greed or what I thought my desire or façade called for at that given moment. Today I'm finding the willingness, with the help of this process, to be more honest with myself. I'm finding that when I'm not deceiving myself, I'm much less inclined to deceive you. The less I deceive you, the less complicated my mind. And if I should deceive you as an uninten-

www.bradleyquick.com

tional automatic response to the information I am receiving, I can always stop, take a deep breath and acknowledge my error. Then I am not only being honest, but I'm also remaining free from having to carry the additional mental and emotional baggage that dishonesty creates. To be honest is to remain free, free from the arrogance that comes with dishonesty. Honesty brings with it humility, and to be humble is to live the truth. That's a good thing.

H.O.W:
Honesty, Open-mindedness, and Willingness. Yes, these substance(s) and/or disorders have become a problem. Yes, I am open-minded enough to realize this method will work for me. Yes, I am willing to do what it takes and work this *Quick Fix Process.* That's the HOW of this process.

Humility:
Being humble, being nonresistant. Understand that you're not always right, and it's OK to be wrong and to have the truth pointed out to you. Being corrected is not a bad thing. Be willing to get off your high horse and listen to another opinion.

I

Insanity:
Simply put, insanity is *doing the same thing over and over again anticipating different results*

Isolation:
Isolation is a state that most of us have experienced unwillingly and, at other times, have resorted to as a protective mechanism. Sometimes we get stuck in isolation for long periods of time. If anyone would have done the things to me that I've done to myself, throughout my life, I would have knocked them out a long time ago. If you're honest, you can probably say the same thing. So why would you want to lock yourself up with yourself, your worst enemy? If I do that, I always lose. If you continue to do that, you'll continue to get the short end of the deal. Go help someone, be of service;

you're needed out there. To isolate yourself now is to deprive yourself of the company of others at the very time you need their company most.

J

Journal:
Your journal is a daily reflection of thoughts, actions, angers, fears, motives, resentments and achievements, put on paper by your own hand, in your own words. This is a way to tally your progress through this wonderful journey called positive change. Also to be put in your journal eventually, by your own hand, are those things that you had planned to take to the grave with you and to share with no one. By doing this exercise, thought to limb, limb to hand, hand to pen, pen to paper, you'll free yourself from those issues or secrets. By revealing yourself, if only to yourself through this positive action, you will be free. It's incredible! When you are done, you can throw that page or those pages away. Remember, we are only as sick as our secrets, so the sooner you look at them and let go of them, the better you will be.

L

Loneliness:
Feeling alone, abandoned, without anyone. At times, our feelings of loneliness are intrusive and all encompassing. We can even feel this terrible emotion when in a crowd surrounded by people. That can feel stronger than when we are actually physically alone. The lonelier I am, the less I'm willing to reach out. The less I reach out, the more lonely I am. It's a classic Catch 22. At times I just can't seem to shake it, other times I can feel more connected by calling someone or reaching out and being of service. Remember, feelings are facts, they are not truths. The fact is, you feel lonely; the truth is, you're only alone with self, and you find yourself bad company. You've got family, you've got friends, you've got coworkers. There are probably

www.bradleyquick.com

a number of different people that would love to hear from you or see you. Loneliness is not a manifestation of actually being alone as much as being dissatisfied with your company, whether you're alone or with others.

M

Mentor:
A mentor is a person that you hold in high regard as having a high level of The Quick Fix, or knowledge as to a particular topic or subject, and one who is willing to share The Quick Fix and knowledge with you. When a potential mentor reaches out, reach back to that person.

N

Necessary:
Needed, a "must have." Working this process, listening to the recorded messages, studying this handbook and experiencing change in your life — all of these are necessary.

Normal:
Conforming your actions to an accepted standard or perceived normality.

P

Phases:
Any stage in a series or cycle of changes. See the *Seven Stages of Development* Chapter.

Pride:
An unduly high opinion of oneself. Satisfaction in something accomplished is good. However, "pride goeth before the fall". Self-admiration, conceit, abundant ego are pride problems. It is good to be proud of what we are doing, and the life-changes that we are initiating and allowing to occur in our daily lives. In these moments of positive self-esteem, we must always remember where we came from and that a sense of humility can only bring us closer to a true understanding of the purpose of our lives.

Promise:
An agreement to do or not to do something. We've all made promises that we've broken, and disappointed many beside ourselves. We are only as good as our word. If you don't mean it, don't say it. If you say it then do it. It's really that simple. The promise here is, if you'll work this, this will work for you.

R

Rejection:
I hate it! There seems to be nothing worse, and it seems to play such a large role in my behavior, especially my behavior towards others. I'm typically in so much fear of being rejected, as if the rejection level regulates my worth as a person, that more times than not, I won't take those actions that may lead to my being rejected. That in itself manipulates my life. I must begin to realize that it is not me that's being rejected, truly. Most often it is my proposal or my opinion, a thought or idea that's being declined, not me as a human being. I'm OK no matter what your reaction to me. I really am, and so are you. It's a constant battle, but I must remember I have value as a person with or without our perceived acceptance or approval

of my advances or proposals, thoughts or ideas. We can only be rejected, if in anticipation, we don't get the outcome we want or expect to get.

Resentment:
To hold on to self-righteous indignation over something or someone. As the word implies, resentment re-lives situations over and over again. Resentments are typically awfully hard for us to let go of. But there is a method for relief, if you're willing to do what it takes. Let me share with you the process for relief, which must be followed to achieve freedom from resentments.

1. Simply write on a piece of paper the name of the person, place, or thing for which you hold the resentment.
2. List the cause of the resentment. A very brief explanation, however it should be precise and to the point.
3. In what ways did this affect you? Did it affect your self-esteem, ambitions, or personal relationships? Or was it your pride, pocketbook, personal security, or sex relations that were affected? Only you can be the honest judge.
4. You must then list your part in this endeavor. (Yes, you did play a part in this.) Were you selfish, self-centered, self-seeking, dishonest or afraid? Put aside for a moment the anger you're feeling towards the resented party, and list your part.

Example:
a. **Name:** Tom.
b. **Cause:** Got the promotion at work.
c. **Affects:** My self-esteem, personal relations, ambitions, fear, and pocketbook.
d. **My Part:** I was *selfish* in thinking I should get the position, he's been with the company longer. I was really *dishonest* with my hours on the time card, and he does generally work harder than I do. I was *afraid* (in fear) of looking bad to my coworkers.

After listing these items on paper, using this format, simply call the Hotline or your mentor, read them aloud ,then throw them away. Be free of these resentments and move on. Remember, it works only if you work it. This process can also be used to rid yourself of those grudges (resentments) you've been carrying around with you since day one. You may not believe it, but they still have a profound impact on you today. All those people who have upset you to no end, those things that still make you feel bad or angry, or those things you should or could have done differently, produce grudges or resentments. Simply make a list and follow the example above and you'll be free. It's a wonderful sensation, a newfound freedom. It's one that you can and should put forth effort to attain.

Rule 62:
Don't take yourself so seriously. There are no big deals! Learn to laugh at yourself and your mistakes.

S

Sad
Unhappy, sorry, dejected, depressed, heartbroken, mourning, grieving, hopeless, or worried. The best way to get out of sadness is to go help someone else do something. Go be of service to others, and by doing so, you will be of service to yourself. Sometimes sadness about loss is appropriate: it's part of the human condition. Learn to differentiate it from self-pity, depression, and the like.

Sanity:
The condition of being sane; healthiness of mind; soundness of judgment; knowing right from wrong, or at least being willing to get a second opinion. Sanity is understanding that you cannot fix your insides with something on the outside, though we have all tried to do this very thing many times with little or no success. You now have an understanding that you cannot mask it, cover it up, avoid it, go around it, or overlook it for long. You now must go through it, whatever it is. The only way beyond it is through it. Once through it, in reflection, you'll realize that it was only a cloud of dust and not the thunderstorm that you perceived it to be.

Security:
Freedom from fear, doubt and self-delusion. Knowing that every-thing is really going to be alright. Having inner peace.

Selfish:
Self-seeking, self-centered, self-indulgent, self-obsessed. Not being concerned with others or only engaging in activities intended to benefit one's self—a self-defeating act.

Self-centered:
Concerned only with one's own affairs; selfish.

Self-delusion:
Self-deception. Not being in touch with reality, making things up and believing them. This is one reason why it is so very important to get a second opinion continuously from an unin-volved third party familiar with this process.

Self-pity:
Pity for oneself, and total self-obsession. This is not a comfortable state to stay in for any length of time. Don't let your ego keep you here; false pride is a killer. Go help somebody, anybody. Get out of yourself. Don't wait, go now and take positive action!

Self-reliance:
Reliance only on one's own powers, judgment, and abilities. Up to this point, for most of us, this has been the case and has led us to our current state of mind and body. To let go of self is to embrace the world. To trust this process is to become free from the bondage of self.

Self-sabotage:
Unintentionally defeating one's own best interest, making deci-sions detrimental to one's own well-being, then wondering why. Limiting self-progression. Associating with, or going to, the same people and places where substance abuse and disorders are prevalent. The same places and people with whom we once felt some association, though detrimental to our well-being.

Self-seeking:
Mainly seeking to further one's own interest. Selfish.

Service:
Helping anyone with anything, anytime. (A great way to get out of yourself. You should pay the recipient for the opportunity.)

Sex:
A physical act of love between two people. A necessity for human-kind's continued existence, not to be taken lightly. Sex can be a beautiful thing, then again it can be very detrimental to our well-being. It can make us believe things that may not be true about ourselves and others. Sex has the ability to make us think that we are emotionally somewhere we are not. Sex is one of the most powerful avoidance mechanisms I have ever experienced. Aside from eating and sleeping, sex is something that all living creatures do, in one form or another, so it can't be all bad. If you think about it, bringing new life into this world is one of the most important aspects of our existence. Again, the sexual act is not to be taken lightly. Be respon-sible, look at your part in all interactions of this sort, and ask yourself: Am I being selfish, dishonest, or inconsiderate? Do I unjustifiably arouse jealousy, suspicion, or bitterness? Is my sexual relationship selfish? Look at your part, and make the decision that you will not fall prey to sexual behavior that is not becoming to you. Whatever that looks like, only you can be the judge in this arena. Remember that sex is beautiful if enjoyed under the right circumstances, and not so beautiful if done for the wrong reasons.

Sleep:
Deep relaxation. In the beginning, sleep may be hard to come by for the very reason that our natural timer, our inner clock, is broken by our substance abuse, and for most of us our inner clock has not been used for a very long time. If you're anything like me, you ingested something to come up, ingested something to maintain, and then ingested something else to come down. We used substances to get up, lay down, relax, sleep, enhance this, relieve that, and so on. Our natural clock has been out of whack for so long, it's going to take awhile to start working properly again, but it will. It just takes some time, that's all. In the meantime, while unable to sleep, study this handbook, listen to *Positive Chat Power*, etc. When you're unable to sleep, do all those things that can be done at that time, all the things that you didn't have a chance to do

today. At sleepless moments like that, it's better to take positive action than to wonder and worry why you can't sleep.

Spirituality:
Being at one with the world and the universe constitutes spirituality. Finding universal truth. Up to this point, most of us have enjoyed distilled spirits, and that's just about as spiritual as many of us ever got. Why do you think alcohol, is called "spirits"? Because it creates fun and enjoyment for most, and lets them forget their worries and concerns for a time. However, there is a profound difference between "spirits" and spirit. One is a temporary solution that leads only to sorrow and misery, while the other glows from the inside. Being spiritual inside creates the true freedom we once sought in a bottle.

Sponsor:
(Coach or Mentor) Someone who has experiences in the recovery, self discovery, transformation process and has been there before you. Someone who can share with you their experience regarding your current situation. The one who has walked the path before you and has found the short cut or the best way through and then out the other side. A person whom you can trust and rely upon to tell you how it is, not necessarily someone who will tell you what you want to hear. Though we generally stick with one true sponsor, coach or mentor at a time, it is not etched in stone that we have to have that one individual forever. Trust that the universe will put the right people, at the right time, in your path. Remember, the best of the best at anything always has a coach or a mentor to guide them and show them the best way to get the best effect. This process is no different!

Support:
Allowing others to voluntarily participate in your well being, or you voluntarily participating in the well being of others.

T

Task:
A piece of work to be done. Some tasks require more effort than others. Doing what's at hand to be done and understanding that all you can do is the task at hand, no more, no less. Just do what's in front of you to be done.

Time:
Every moment there has ever been or ever will be. There is nothing but right now, and then right now, and then right now. Stay in the moment and realize that your life is right now. Using this *Quick Fix Process,* over time, you, your life and your relationships will only get better. By not utilizing these methods, over time, life for you may just get worse, and that's a bad time.

Trudge:
To walk one step at a time, confident of your destination and your purpose. Walking through all that life dishes out without losing the vision.

W

Willingness:
Enthusiasm, zeal, readiness and eagerness to comply with the trials and tribulations that come with change. The ability to do whatever it takes to achieve one's goals and ambitions. Acceptance coupled with action.

www.bradleyquick.com

CONCORDANCE   www.bradleyquick.com

A

Abandon; also Abandonment
Page(s): 120

Fear of *Abandonment*
Page(s): 120

Reckless *Abandon* of the Truth
Page(s): 128

The *Abandonment*, the Guilt and the Loss
Page(s): 1

To *Abandon* these Principles
Page(s): 55

You would Certainly *Abandon* Me
Page(s): 7

Abuse; also see Substance Abuse

Constant or Consistent Self-*Abuse*
Page(s): 46

Many of Us use and *Abuse* and Act Out
Page(s): 77

So, Along Come our Fixes, Whatever Substances We *Abuse*
Page(s): 103

To Avoid the Impact of the Newness of Life without *Abuse*
Page(s): 98

We Must Use and *Abuse* our Substance(s) or Disorders in Order to Deal With
Page(s): 77

We Often Have a Tendency to take For Granted and *Abuse* our Body
Page(s): 117

Abusing

Physical and Mental Effects of *Abusing*
Page(s): 18

Abusive

*Also see Resources Section

Total Acceptance
Page(s): 56

Accident

Auto *Accident*
Page(s): 5

Bad *Accident*
Page(s): 3

Bike *Accident*
Page(s): ix, 2

"Why do you Think they Call it An *Accident*?"
Page(s): 31

You Didn't Get in an Accident
Page(s): 64

Action

Acceptance Coupled with *Action*
Page(s): 139

Before Taking *Action*
Page(s): 91

Contrary *Action*
Page(s): 88

Into Positive *Action*
Page(s): 34, 57, 112

Is this *Action* Based on Self
Page(s): 92

Is this *Action* I'm about to Take Based On the Needs of Others
Page(s): 92

Life Changing *Action*
Page(s): 82

Mode of *Action* is the Same for All of These Meds
Page(s): 22

CONCORDANCE

www.bradleyquick.com

*Also see Resources Section

Addict

Addiction(s)*

*Also see Resources Section

Addictive Behavior

ADHD

Admit

Affirmations

CONCORDANCE   www.bradleyquick.com

CONCORDANCE

www.bradleyquick.com

149

C O N C O R D A N C E

www.bradleyquick.com

Allergic

Allergic to Sugar (Everyone is Sensitive to Sugar to Some Extent)
Page(s): 101

Allergies
Page(s): 21

Alone

Actually Being *Alone*
Page(s): 132

Alone we Fall Right Back into Destruction
Page(s): 51

Because of that Fact *Alone* We are Subject To
Page(s): 115

Begin by Listening, Quiet and *Alone*
Page(s): 83

Feeling *Alone*, Abandoned, Without Anyone
Page(s): 131

Feeling Deserted and Left *Alone*
Page(s): 120

I Hadn't Even Left the Dinner Table, Let *Alone* Set the Glass Down
Page(s): 13

I was *Alone* Again and Stuck with Myself
Page(s): xvi

Isolated and *Alone*
Page(s): 7

Listen, Quiet and *Alone*
Page(s): 83

That *Alone* is Going to Take Immense Faith and Courage
Page(s): 31

That *Alone* will Work Wonders
Page(s): 125

Ambition

Amphetamines

Anger; also see Angry

Angry

CONCORDANCE www.bradleyquick.com

Anti Depressants; also Selective Serotonin Reuptake Inhibitors (SSRI's), MAO Inhibitors, Tricyclics

Anxiety:* also see Fear, Worry

CONCORDANCE   www.bradleyquick.com

Assume (Makes an ASS of U and ME)

CONCORDANCE www.bradleyquick.com

Attitude

Automatic Conditioned Response(s)

Avoidance

CONCORDANCE   www.bradleyquick.com

CONCORDANCE

www.bradleyquick.com

CONCORDANCE

www.bradleyquick.com

The Clarity Needed to Avoid the *Bad* Pitches
Page(s): 54

They Called me Big *Bad* Brad
Page(s): 2

The Only Time Such Eating Feels *Bad*
Page(s): 100

This Results in a *Bad* Night's Sleep
Page(s): 102

Those things that Still Make You Feel *Bad*
Page(s): 97, 135

"Unknowns" are Not Necessarily Good or *Bad*
Page(s): 62

We all Have our *Bad* Moments
Page(s): 55

Will only Prolong Your Agony and Bring You *Bad* Results
Page(s): 39

You are Not a Weak or "*Bad*" Person
Page(s): 111

You find Yourself *Bad* Company
Page(s): 131

Barbiturates

Barbiturates are Another Kind of Drug that Produce Similar Effects
Page(s): 25

Barbiturates have Been the Leading Cause of Death
Page(s): 25

Heroin to *Barbiturates*, Chocolate to Caramel, Marlboros to Winston
Page(s): 48

Includes *Barbiturates*, Such As
Page(s): 24

Behavior

CONCORDANCE

www.bradleyquick.com

Behavioral Disorder(s)

CONCORDANCE   www.bradleyquick.com

www.bradleyquick.com

*Also see Resources Section

CONCORDANCE

www.bradleyquick.com

*Also see Resources Section

We Can Make New and *Better* Knowns for You
Page(s): 63

Showed Me the Way to *Better* Living*
Page(s): 3

Get a *Better* Perspective of My Life
Page(s): 87

Better Posture
Page(s): 113

We invent *Better* Scenarios
Page(s): 59

Make Up your Mind that Tomorrow Will Be a *Better* Day
Page(s): 85

Move *Better*
Page(s): 113

Much Better

It's a **Much Better** Way to Go
Page(s): 14

Will Get Along **Much Better** if I Just Stick To
Page(s): 33

You Will Feel so **Much Better** as a Result
Page(s): 100

You'll Have a **Much Better** Chance of Living Without It
Page(s): 34

Think *Better*
Page(s): 102

We Must Change our Internal Programming for the *Better* From
Within
Page(s): 62

You'll Be a *Better* Person for It
Page(s): 125

Body; also see Body and Mind

Body and Mind

CONCORDANCE www.bradleyquick.com

CONCORDANCE

www.bradleyquick.com

Business

Became Consciously Aware and Went on About your *Business*
Page(s): 64

Business Law Became Appealing
Page(s): 7

He had Hoped He Could Spark my *Business* Interest
Page(s): 4

I am in the Efforts *Business*, Not the Results *Business*
Page(s): 87

We are in the Efforts *Business*, Not the Results *Business*
Page(s): 123

We're in the Efforts *Business* Not the Results *Business*
Page(s): xiii

You are in the Efforts *Business*, not the Results *Business*
Page(s): 33, 84

C

Cause and Effect

Cause and Effect within Our Bodies
Page(s): 19, 26

Familiar with the Phrase *"Cause and Effect"*
Page(s): 32

Fully Understand the Feeling or Emotion (*Cause and Effect*)
Page(s): 91

So When you Combine Distorted "Cause and Effect" with
Page(s): 32

Central Nervous System (CNS)

Alcohol Attacks the *CNS*, Liver, Kidneys, Heart and
Page(s): 20

CONCORDANCE   www.bradleyquick.com

www.bradleyquick.com

*Also see Resources Section

Common

www.bradleyquick.com

CONCORDANCE   www.bradleyquick.com

Conditions

Conscious Mind

*Also see Resources Section

Courage

Cravings

CONCORDANCE www.bradleyquick.com

D

Daily

A *Daily* Reprieve
Page(s): 87

Daily Activity
Page(s): 92

Daily Allowance
Page(s): 100

Daily at A Steady P.A.C.E.
Page(s): 95

Daily Health Booster
Page(s): 109

Daily Journal
Page(s): 85, 90, 95, 96, 97

Daily Rituals
Page(s): 88

Daily Life Experiences
Page(s): 91

Daily Living
Page(s): 129

Daily Supplement
Page(s): 100

Daily Tasks
Page(s): 89, 90

Exercise *Daily*
Page(s): 84

Listen *Daily*
Page(s): 83

On a *Daily* Basis
Page(s): 61, 82, 95, 101

CONCORDANCE

www.bradleyquick.com

Death

CONCORDANCE   www.bradleyquick.com

Detoxifying

Development

Diet; also see Method of Eating

*Also see Resources Section

Direction

*Also see Resources Section

Discouraged

Discover; also see Uncover Discover and Discard

Disease

Dis-ease

Like a Disease (*Dis-ease*)
Page(s): 45

Dishonest; also see Dishonesty

Am I Being Selfish, *Dishonest*, or Inconsiderate?
Page(s): 137

I Was Really *Dishonest*
Page(s): 97, 134

Selfish, Self-centered, Self-seeking, *Dishonest,* or Afraid
Page(s): 96

Dishonesty; also see Dishonest, Honesty
Page(s): 124

Are Common Examples of *Dishonesty*
Page(s): 124

Dishonesty Brings with it Arrogance, Treachery
Page(s): 124

Free from the Arrogance that Comes with *Dishonesty*
Page(s): 130

Mental and Emotional Baggage that *Dishonesty* Creates
Page(s): 130

Self-preservation, Self-pity, Deceit, *Dishonesty*, Guilt or Shame?
Page(s): 125

Disorder(s)

Behavioral *Disorders* do have Many Similarities
Page(s): xvii

Bipolar *Disorder*
Page(s): 105

Disorder *Free*
Page(s): 36, 52, 53, 92

Emotional *Disorders*
Page(s): 28

Divorce

Dopamine

CONCORDANCE   www.bradleyquick.com

*Also see Resources Section

CONCORDANCE

www.bradleyquick.com

*Also see Resources Section

Drunk*

Dysfunction

www.bradleyquick.com

E

Easier

Effort(s)

CONCORDANCE   www.bradleyquick.com

*Also see Resources Section

CONCORDANCE

www.bradleyquick.com

*Also see Resources Section

Emotions*

CONCORDANCE

www.bradleyquick.com

*Also see Resources Section

CONCORDANCE www.bradleyquick.com

www.bradleyquick.com

*Also see Resources Section

Expectation(s)

CONCORDANCE   www.bradleyquick.com

CONCORDANCE

www.bradleyquick.com

*Also see Resources Section

Explore

We Must *Explore* our Similarities More than Our Differences
Page(s): xvii

F

Facade
Page(s): 127

What I thought My Desire or *Facade* Called For
Page(s): 129

Fact(s); also Factors

After the *Fact*
Page(s): 10, 60

A True *Fact* Is that You Do Feel the Way You Feel
Page(s): 79

Because of That *Fact* Alone we Are Subject To
Page(s): 115

Feelings are *Facts* they are Not Truths
Page(s): 36, 131

In *Fact*
Page(s): 4, 9, 15, 22, 40, 42, 43, 60, 100

Other *Factors*
Page(s): 78

Risk *Factors*
Page(s): 20

Some *Fact* of Our Lives Unacceptable to Us
Page(s): 120

Then there's the *Fact* that Some of us May Be
Page(s): 101

Unique Identifying *Factors*
Page(s): 117

*Also see Resources Section

Faith
Page(s): 126

CONCORDANCE

www.bradleyquick.com

*Also see Resources Section

Just Have *Faith* in This Process
Page(s): 31

Letting Go of Control and Having *Faith*
Page(s): 123

This *Faith* Must be Accompanied by Trust
Page(s): 32

We must Have *Faith* in Something Other than Ourselves
Page(s): 126

We must Rely On, and Have *Faith* in, This Process
Page(s): 35

Family*

A *Family* History of Addictive Behaviors
Page(s): 20

Got Most of the Attention from My Parents, Grandparents and Relatives
Page(s): 2

Before the Separation of *Family* and/or Friends
Page(s): 43

Come and Spend the Holiday with the *Family*
Page(s): 8

Friends and *Family*, Sometimes, Must Delicately Maneuver Themselves Around You
Page(s): 90

I Saw the Disgust in the Eyes of My *Family* Members
Page(s): 8

If you Have a *Family* History of Substance Abuse
Page(s): 112

It is Always those Closest to Us, our *Family* and Friends
Page(s): 6

Knowing I would Be Confronted by *Family*
Page(s): 8

My *Family* and Friends Suffered the Most
Page(s): 121

Now My *Family* and Friends Benefit from My Existence
Page(s): 121

So My Half Brother Could Meet the Quick *Family*
Page(s): 8

"Substance Abuse Runs in My *Family* So I Can't help It."
Page(s): 112

The Second Eldest in a *Family* of Nine
Page(s): 1

This is Not About Race or *Family* of Origin
Page(s): 51

You've got *Family*, You've got Friends and Coworkers
Page(s): 131

F.A.S.T. - (Faith, Acceptance, Service, This too shall pass)
Page(s): 37, 81, 99

The *F.A.S.T.* C.L.E.A.N. P.A.C.E. for Positive Change
Page(s): 30

Fault

I Know None of this Is Your *Fault*
Page(s): 31

I Reported this Accident as Not Being My *Fault*
Page(s): 31

I Was Convinced that His Death was My *Fault*
Page(s): 2

I will Not Find *Fault* with Anyone or Anything
Page(s): 86

It was Always Someone Else's *Fault*, Never my Own
Page(s): 31

Slow to Ever Admit to Any *Fault* of my Own
Page(s): 31

The *Fault* of Another
Page(s): 45

www.bradleyquick.com

Fix

CONCORDANCE   www.bradleyquick.com

CONCORDANCE

www.bradleyquick.com

*Also see Resources Section

*Also see Resources Section

Fish, Poultry, Lean Meat (*Free* Range)
Page(s): 110

Follow the Example above and You Can be *Free*
Page(s): 97

Follow the Example Above and You'll be *Free*
Page(s): 135

Follow this Same Process and Be *Free*
Page(s): 49

Free from that First Drink, Puff, Pill, Bite, Act, or Whatever
Page(s): 38

Free from the Arrogance that Comes with Dishonesty
Page(s): 130

I Must Stay Substance and Disorder *Free*
Page(s): 38

If I Stay Substance Abuse *Free* Just in this Moment
Page(s): 38

Just for Right Now, in this Moment to Be *Free*
Page(s): 56

Letting Someone Else Live rent *Free* Between Your Ears
Page(s): 96

Live Life to its Fullest as a *Free* and Unencumbered Individual
Page(s): 77

Once You are Substance Abuse and Behavioral Disorder *Free*
Page(s): 54

People Get *Free*, Forget where They Came From, and Stop Doing
Page(s): 55

Restore and Maintain Your Brain function and Remain Substance
Abuse *Free*
Page(s): 109

Substance Abuse *Free* One Day at a Time
Page(s): 38

The Easier it is to Set Yourself *Free*
Page(s): 99

*Also see Resources Section

*Also see Resources Section

Friend(s)

Friendship; see Love

Frustration

Fun

Death would Have Been More *Fun*
Page(s): 16

Going on a Relaxing, *Fun* loving, Guided Journey
Page(s): 69

It Could Have Been *Fun* in the Beginning
Page(s): xvii

G

Guarantee
Page(s): 53

Guarantee you Bad Results
Page(s): 53

I can Personally *Guarantee* This
Page(s): 87

My *Guarantee* is That
Page(s): 53

That's My *Guarantee* to You
Page(s): 53

That's the *Guarantee*
Page(s): 53

God

I Felt Like a *God* for the Duration of that Rush
Page(s): 9

I had No Concept of *God*
Page(s): 15

I Have Found my *God*, my Work, and my Purpose
Page(s): 58

I Prayed to this Thing Called *God* but They Died Anyway
Page(s): 15

CONCORDANCE   www.bradleyquick.com

I was *God* and John Holmes
Page(s): 9

They Where also Talking all this Nonsense About *God*
Page(s): 15

Good; also see Good News

A Body that Feels and Looks *Good*
Page(s): 101

A Very *Good* Thing
Page(s): 127

Avoid the Bad Pitches and Hit the *Good* Ones
Page(s): 54

Because it Tastes *Good*
Page(s): 101

Better than, or Not as *Good* as We Should Be
Page(s): 40

Bringing us More Harm and Distress than *Good*
Page(s): 80

Consumption of Anything that Made Me Feel *Good*
Page(s): 9

Dependent on the Drug to Produce *Good* Feelings
Page(s): 23

Edging *Good* Out
Page(s): 125

"Feel *Good*" or "Pick Me Up" Drug
Page(s): 23

For *Good* Measure
Page(s): 11, 86

Good Cause, *Good* Effect
Page(s): 32

Good Intent
Page(s): 63

CONCORDANCE   www.bradleyquick.com

*Also see Resources Section

CONCORDANCE www.bradleyquick.com

*Also see Resources Section

Guilt

Guilty

H

Habits

H.A.L.T. - (Hungry Angry Lonely & Tired)

Happiness;* also see Happy

Happy*

It's About Being *Happy*
Page(s): 51

Inner Child, *Happy* Past
Page(s): 64, 65, 76

I Will Be *Happy*
Page(s): 86

Made up My Mind to Be *Happy*
Page(s): 86

We Could Not Be *Happy*
Page(s): 120

Harmful Disorders

Find Something Other than Our Harmful Disorders to Rely Upon
Page(s): 39

Hatred: see Anger

Hate, also see Resentment

Am I Wallowing in *Hate*
Page(s): 91

Fear and Control Bring with Them Disappointment, Envy, *Hate*, and Rage
Page(s): 87

How Often are You in *Hate*, Love, Fear, Jealousy or Envy?
Page(s): 78

I *Hate* it
Page(s): 133

In Hate, in Love, or in Fear
Page(s): 8

Head; also see Self

Back Up into Your *Head*
Page(s): 68

By Shaking Your *Head* from Side to Side, Indicating, "No
Page(s): 38

CONCORDANCE   www.bradleyquick.com

Gonna Hit You Right in the *Head*
Page(s): 32

I Don't have to Listen to what My *Head* is Saying
Page(s): 50

I Now Automatically Shake My Head "No."
Page(s): 38

In Your *Head* you've Already Been
Page(s): 60

Just by Shaking Your *Head* "No!"
Page(s): 38

My *Head* Grew to the Point that I Could Not Get Thru the Door
Page(s): x

My *Head* Said that I was Going there For one Reason
Page(s): 38

No Matter what My Head Tells Me
Page(s): 16

Shake Your *Head* "No," Reinforcing Your Determination
Page(s): 39

She was In My *Head* Throughout the Day
Page(s): 59

We'll be all right, no Matter what Our *Head* Says
Page(s): 39

Your Ability to Hold Your *Head* Up
Page(s): 27

Healthy

A Lot, a Little, *Healthy* and Not so *Healthy*
Page(s): 99

Healthy and Physically Fit
Page(s): 55

Healthy Brain, *Healthy* Mind, *Healthy* Purpose
Page(s): 103

www.bradleyquick.com

CONCORDANCE

www.bradleyquick.com

Higher Power; also see Faith, Prayer

Holistic

Honest; also see Honesty

CONCORDANCE www.bradleyquick.com

Honesty

Hope

CONCORDANCE

www.bradleyquick.com

Hopeless

CONCORDANCE www.bradleyquick.com

It Seems to Be a Very *Hopeless* State
Page(s): 120

Leaving us *Hopeless*, Helpless and Different from the Rest
Page(s): 120

Living in This *Hopeless* and Helpless State
Page(s): 16

More *Hopeless* and Helpless Than Before
Page(s): 55

Recovered From a *Hopeless* and Helpless State of Body and Mind
Page(s): xvi

Their Seemingly *Hopeless* State of Body and Mind
Page(s): 35

Hotline
Page(s): 96, 97, 134

24-Hour Alcohol and Drug Help Line
(800)448-3000

24-Hour National Depression *Hotline*
(800) 242-2211

24-Hour Suicide *Hotline*
(800) 784-2433

H.O.W. - (Honesty, Open-mindedness & Willingness)
Page(s): 39, 130

Humble; also see Humility

Being *Humble*, Being Nonresistant
Page(s): 130

Be *Humble* in Receiving their Answer
Page(s): 54

The Willingness to Be Honest and *Humble*
Page(s): 84

To Remain *Humble* to its Purpose
Page(s): 17

CONCORDANCE

www.bradleyquick.com

Humility

Honesty Brings with it *Humility*
Page(s): 130

Humility: Being Humble, Being Nonresistant
Page(s): 130

Humility Can only Bring Us closer to a True Understanding
Page(s): 133

I Always Got Up, Dusted off the *Humility*
Page(s): x

I

Indecision

I will Save Myself from Two Pests: Hurry and *Indecision*
Page(s): 87

Identify; also Identifying

Every One of Us has Unique *Identifying* Factors
Page(s): 117

Identify with at Least Some of It
Page(s): 17

Inhabitants

About the World and its *Inhabitants*
Page(s): 13

How the World and All of its *Inhabitants* Should Act
Page(s): 115

Give it Back to the Universe and All its *Inhabitants*
Page(s): 57

CONCORDANCE   www.bradleyquick.com

*Also see Resources Section

Inner Clock

Our *Inner Clock* Has not Been Used for a Very Long Time
Page(s): 137

Our *Inner Clock*, is Broken
Page(s): 137

Inner Peace

Finding *Inner Peace*
Page(s): 64, 65, 76

Having *Inner Peace*
Page(s): 136

Inner Peace, Tranquility, Serenity
Page(s): 55

Inner Program

Self-preservation by Your *Inner Program*
Page(s): 62

The Subconscious Mind (Your *Inner Program*)
Page(s): 83

Inner Self

See and feel My *Inner Self*
Page(s): 11

Inspiration; also see Inspired

As you Enter an *Inspired* State
Page(s): 67

As you Have Now Entered an *Inspired* State
Page(s): 69

Feel more Comfortable and *Inspired*
Page(s): 66

For Days, Weeks and Months, I was *Inspired*
Page(s): x

*Also see Resources Section

Inspired

www.bradleyquick.com

CONCORDANCE www.bradleyquick.com

CONCORDANCE

www.bradleyquick.com

K

L

*Also see Resources Section

Being Happy and Contented with *Life*
Page(s): 51

Best to Get Through This Moment in *Life*
Page(s): 121

Be Willing to Accept This Positive Change into Your *Life*
Page(s): 70

Bringing New *Life* into This World
Page(s): 137

Buffered Me From *Life*, Helped Me to Fit In
Page(s): 4

Came into My *Life*, Wanting Nothing
Page(s): iii

Change, Motivation and *Life* Enhancement
Page(s): xi

Conducive to *Life* as We Know It
Page(s): 115

Dealing With My *Life*
Page(s): 14

Deal with *Life* As it Presents Itself
Page(s): 47

Defiance of Boundaries Became a Way of *Life*
Page(s): 4

Denying This Issue in Your *Life*
Page(s): 56

Devotion to Working *Life* Enhancement Processes
Page(s): 103

Ending up On Skid Row, and All My *Life* Experiences in Between
Page(s): ix

Enhance Positive Change in Your *Life*
Page(s): 57

Erratic Behavior and Substance Abuse Continued to Be the Focus of
My *Life*
Page(s): 57

*Also see Resources Section

www.bradleyquick.com

*Also see Resources Section

*Also see Resources Section

*Also see Resources Section

CONCORDANCE

www.bradleyquick.com

257

CONCORDANCE

www.bradleyquick.com

*Also see Resources Section

List

CONCORDANCE

www.bradleyquick.com

*Also see Resources Section

LSD

Loss

Love*

CONCORDANCE   www.bradleyquick.com

Lonely

*Also see Resources Section

M

Magic

Maintain

www.bradleyquick.com

*Also see Resources Section

*Also see Resources Section

*Also see Resources Section

www.bradleyquick.com

*Also see Resources Section

Resentment: A Thought Continuously Resent through the *Mind*
Page(s): 96, 122

Seemingly Hopeless State of Body and *Mind*
Page(s): 35, 77

Serenity and Soundness of *Mind*
Page(s): 55

"Sharpen" our *Mind* and Raise our Energy Level
Page(s): 103

So Make up Your *Mind* to Feel Better
Page(s): 102

Take the Body, the *Mind* will Follow
Page(s): 30

The Condition of Being Sane; Healthiness of *Mind*
Page(s): 135

The Less I Deceive You, the Less Complicated My *Mind*
Page(s): 129

The *Mind* Altering Substance Nicotine
Page(s): 98

The *Mind* Can Conceive
Page(s): 26

The *Mind* is Divided into Three Sections
Page(s): 61

To Sustain a Healthy Body and *Mind*
Page(s): 100

To Restore the *Mind* to its Full Potential
Page(s): 78

Today I have Made up My *Mind* to be Happy
Page(s): 86

Undesired Behavior Comes into My *Mind*
Page(s): 38

When Your *Mind* is Clouded
Page(s): 122

Miracles

www.bradleyquick.com

*Also see Resources Section

Moment; also This Moment

CONCORDANCE

www.bradleyquick.com

*Also see Resources Section

Nor the *Moment* that Will Never Be Again
Page(s): 91

One *Moment* at a Time

Every Moment, **One *Moment* at a Time**
Page(s): 33

Live through This Day Only, **One *Moment* at a Time**
Page(s): 86

You Can Do this **One *Moment* at a Time**
Page(s): 42

Put Aside for a *Moment* the Anger You're Feeling
Page(s): 96, 134

The *Moment* you Realize that Your Actions, Beliefs, and Motives Change for the Worse
Page(s): 122

Stay in the *Moment*
Page(s): 38

I am Now Able to **Stay in the *Moment***
Page(s): 70, 71, 72

I Must **Stay in the *Moment***
Page(s): 122

Stay in the *Moment* and Realize that Your Life is Right Now
Page(s): 139

Take a *Moment*
Page(s): 48

Take a *Moment* and Reflect
Page(s): 42

Take a *Moment* and Share What You've Written
Page(s): 95

Take a *Momen*t for Yourselves and Do what You Feel Like Doing
Page(s): 75

Let's **Take a *Momen*t** and Talk About our Planet.
Page(s): 115

*Also see Resources Section

www.bradleyquick.com

*Also see Resources Section

More

www.bradleyquick.com

www.bradleyquick.com

*Also see Resources Section

More often than Not (Even when reporting what I Thought to Be the Truth)
Page(s): 129

More often Times than Not
Page(s): v

More Times than Not, I won't Take those Actions
Page(s): 133

More Times than Not, it's At a Much Quicker
Page(s): 55

My Answer was Always, "*More*."
Page(s): 10

More Times than Not Blurred by Other Factors
Page(s): 78

More Times than Not, Inner Peace
Page(s): 55

More Times than Not, our Reactions Left a Lot to Be Desired
Page(s): 79

More Willingness
Page(s): 58, 87

Much faster and *More* Profound Results
Page(s): 61

My Perception has Been, sometimes *More* than Others
Page(s): 115

Neither any *More*, Nor Any Less Gravity would Be Conducive
Page(s): 115

No *More* Thinking to it, Now it's Time to Just Go Do it
Page(s): 84

No *More* Using and/or Abusing
Page(s): 49

Now Go Help Somebody and Strive to Achieve *More*
Page(s): 120

On *More* than One Occasion Without His Pills
Page(s): 49

CONCORDANCE

www.bradleyquick.com

*Also see Resources Section

CONCORDANCE

www.bradleyquick.com

*Also see Resources Section

Morphine

Motive; also see Motives

Motives

Mph

My Part

Myth(s)

*Also see Resources Section

N

Narcotic*

Natural Mind

CHAPTER 9

Feelings and Emotions

We begin by looking at feelings and emotions. Feelings and emotions are big reasons why so many of us use and abuse and act out. These feelings and emotions have been avoided by most of us throughout the years. Let's start by looking and categorizing these emotions:

Happy
Sad
Excited
Depressed
Angry
Fear
Hate
Love

I personally have recovered from a seemingly hopeless state of body and mind, and have seen thousands of others recover from substance abuse and disorders of all types using the *Quick Fix Process* and other methods like it. Understand, believe and take it to heart, and the direct result will be a chance for you to live life to its fullest as a free and unencumbered individual.

Let's define what exactly it is we're referring to when we say feelings and emotions.

Feelings: possessing great sensibility; easily moved; perception by the senses.

Emotions: any specific feeling; any of various complex reactions with both mental and physical manifestations.

www.bradleyquick.com

www.bradleyquick.com

NOTE

The first part of the *feelings* definition reads, "possessing great sensibility". This is the truth, taken to the extreme, for most of us. Hypersensitivity, overreaction, or whatever you wish to call this "great sensibility," seems to be a very common trait among us. We amplify perceived reality. I've certainly done a good job of this, how about you?

Feelings is also defined as, "easily moved." I think this refers to our mood changes, or mood swings. If you think about it, how many times in a 24-hour day are you happy, sad, excited, depressed, or angry? How often are you in hate, love, fear, jealousy or envy? Quite a few, I'll bet! I think you'll agree that rapid and dramatic changes in our moods are common occurrences, some days more than others. Let us just agree that our moods fluctuate greatly, sometimes even severely. You may be thinking, "Not me, this doesn't apply to me." Don't be defiant. Remember, looking for the similarities, not the differences, is what will help you.

Finally, *feelings* can be termed, "perception by the senses." This may be the most accurate or applicable part of the *feelings* definition.

Perception: "How our senses perceive (or believe) the world (to be) around us." Our perception is more times than not blurred by other factors. It is distorted easily by feelings that may or may not be true. Thus far, your best thinking has got you all messed up! Your beliefs, thoughts, ideas and interpretations of reality and the world around you may not all be true. But you believe them anyway. I'm sure you would agree that your perception is and has been somewhat distorted from time to time. Consequently, we must change our thoughts, ideals and beliefs, so as to correct our perception and to restore the mind to its full potential. Self-delusion can get pretty bad, especially if you are hungry, angry, lonely and/or tired, or filled with envy or fear. They all affect and influence our mind's perception, sometimes distorting it to the extreme. Remember, all of this amounts to our reactions or our *emotions.*

Emotions are defined as any specific feeling. "Any of various complex reactions with both mental and physical manifestations." This translates as to how we react both mentally and physically to various perceived stimuli. Do you react out of fear of loss or adverse consequence? Pain or pleasure? Is your immediate response one of self-preservation, self-pity, deceit, dishonesty, guilt or shame? Think about it, because you'll have to answer these questions for yourself.

Up to this point, our perception has been extremely distorted and our reactions have often times been most inappropriate. More times than not, our reactions left a lot to be desired. If you're anything like me you've regretted, admittedly or not, most if not all of your inappropriate reactions to life, especially when they concern others.

The bottom line is this: our reactions to those perceptions cause us to engage in substance abuse and behavioral disorders. Having gotten to the point of relying on something from the outside (substances, behaviors, etc.) to fix our insides (feelings and emotions) is a death sentence for most of us. It is nothing but prolonged agony at best.

If you are currently suffering as a result of using and abusing, and have not yet fallen to the level of prolonged agony, don't worry, it's only a matter of time before you do drop to this dreadful state. Why not just stop now? You hit bottom the moment you quit digging. Together we can win, we really can!

Feelings are facts, therefore they are not truths. The fact is, you feel the way you feel, even though your perception certainly may not be, and probably isn't, an accurate reflection of reality. Feelings are facts, not truths. *A* true fact is that you do feel

NOTE
_____

www.bradleyquick.com

www.bradleyquick.com

                NOTE
----

the way you feel. But, don't blindly accept those feelings as *the* truth of the matter.

Remember that whatever the emotion or feeling, our solution, up to this point, has been to change how we feel through our substance(s) and/or behaviors. Now this fix-all is not fixing anything, any longer. Now that our using and abusing fix-all is bringing us more harm and distress than good, it's time to put it to bed, once and for all.

Quick Fix Tools

The Quick Fix Process
(F.A.S.T. C.L.E.A.N. P.A.C.E.)

"There is a principle which is a bar against all information, which is proof against all arguments and which cannot fail to keep a man in everlasting ignorance — that principle is contempt prior to investigation."

Herbert Spencer

This process, if followed, will change your life. The more you follow this process, the more you will have a newfound set of coping mechanisms, and the better your life will become. The better your life becomes, the better is the world, and so on. Remember, today you have the ability to accept the things you cannot change, you have the courage to change the things you can, and you have the wisdom to know the difference.

Here is where the work begins. Remember, you had to work to learn to ride a bike, drive a car, or ski the slopes. Once we've learned these processes, they come to us as second nature, without real thought. These are called *automatic conditioned responses*. The *Quick Fix Process* will work the same way. For some of you, it may be somewhat of a struggle at first, a real challenge. Then, as you continue to work it in all aspects of your life, it becomes an *automatic conditioned response*.

www.bradleyquick.com

www.bradleyquick.com

NOTE

I'm sure that you will agree with me that when we make up our minds to do something, there is usually no stopping us until we either succeed, fizzle out, or move on to something else, right? This process is the same way. None of us have failed while truly working, studying and living this *Quick Fix Process* on a daily basis. We must continue to read the *Daily Affirmations*, live the *Quick 10,* make the proper phone calls or contacts, and do whatever else is necessary to remain free from substances and disorders for *"just right now."* (Snap your fingers and say, *Just Right Now!*) On the other hand, many of us have failed and fallen right back into abusing substances and/or abusive behaviors because we did not continue to do all it takes to remain free *in this moment.* That's right, this moment, no more no less. In *just this moment,* you must do all it takes to remain free. And the good news is that you're capable and in control of doing all that needs to be done in this moment to remain free.

I know through my firsthand experience that you can do this. By simply taking the following positive life changing action on a daily basis, you can and will become the best you've ever been. I promise!

Your Life Changing Agenda

A. Read this handbook daily. Start by reading the whole book from cover to cover, along the way highlighting everything that makes sense to you and everything that you have questions about. Then read it again. While reading these pages, make the decision that you're ready for positive change, that you will adopt and apply these thoughts, ideas and methods into your daily life. This will begin to enhance change for you.

Nicotine also Causes an Initial Stimulation
Page(s): 27

Or Heroin and *Nicotine* to Take Us away From it All
Page(s): 103

The Mind altering Substance *Nicotine*
Page(s): 98

To Continue to Ingest this Narcotic *Nicotine*
Page(s): 99

Nobody

Like that Elephant *Nobody* has Admitted is Standing in the Middle of
the Room
Page(s): 46

Nobody Meant to Do It
Page(s): 31

No Matter What

I'm OK *No Matter What* Your Reaction to Me
Page(s): 133

No Matter What My Head Tells Me
Page(s): 16

No Matter What our Head Says
Page(s): 39

Remain Free From Substance Abuse and Behavioral Disorders, *No Matter What*
Page(s): 94

Won't Give in to My Substance(s), *No Matter What*
Page(s): 16

You'll be Just Fine *No Matter What* Your Head Says
Page(s): 92

Now; also see Just Right Now!

Accept this Positive Change into Your Life *Now*
Page(s): 70, 71

CONCORDANCE

www.bradleyquick.com

CONCORDANCE   www.bradleyquick.com

*Also see Resources Section

*Also see Resources Section

CONCORDANCE

www.bradleyquick.com

*Also see Resources Section

O

Obsession

Total Self *Obsession*

Ocean

CONCORDANCE www.bradleyquick.com

Our Disorders; also Your Disorders

Oxygen

P

Pace

P.A.C.E. - (Positive Action Cures Everything)

CONCORDANCE

www.bradleyquick.com

Pain; also see Trouble

CONCORDANCE   www.bradleyquick.com

Parents*

Party; also Partying

Paralyzed

Peace of Mind; see Serenity

*Also see Resources Section

Perception

CONCORDANCE

www.bradleyquick.com

*Also see Resources Section

Perfectionism

Perfect

CONCORDANCE www.bradleyquick.com

Perfectness

Peripheral Nervous System (PNS)

Phases (Any stage in a series or cycle of changes)

Planet (Earth); also see World

A Small Body of Water Covering two Thirds the Face of the *Planet*
Page(s): 116

Breathing Creature on the Face of the *Planet*
Page(s): 116

Hedonistic, Emotionally Driven Animals on this *Planet*
Page(s): 118

If during this 67,000 mph Orbit Around the Sun this *Planet*
Page(s): 116

If every Living Thing on the Face of this *Planet*, Microorganism to Elephant
Page(s): 117

If this Beautiful *Planet* of Ours were to Sway one Inch Closer
Page(s): 116

Let's Take a Moment and Talk about Our *Planet*
Page(s): 115

Living Creature on the Face of the *Planet*, Exhales (Carbon Dioxide)
Page(s): 116

Perfect Gravitational Pull on the Face of this Beautiful *Planet*
Page(s): 115

The Most Important Person on the Face of the *Planet* is Reading this Sentence
Page(s): 53

The Strange Things that Happen on Our *Planet*
Page(s): 116

This *Planet* is Also Tilted to One Side on a 23.45 Degree Axis
Page(s): 115

This *Planet* is Spinning Around at Approximately 1,000 mph
Page(s): 115

We, Along with Everything Else on the *Planet*
Page(s): 115

While this Beautiful *Planet* of Ours is Spinning Around
Page(s): 116

CONCORDANCE   www.bradleyquick.com

Pleasure

Positive Action; also see Positive Thinking

www.bradleyquick.com

*Also see Resources Section

Positive Change; also see Positive Action

www.bradleyquick.com

*Also see Resources Section

CONCORDANCE

www.bradleyquick.com

CONCORDANCE   www.bradleyquick.com

My Ego and Delusional *Pride* Took Off
Page(s): x

My fragile Ego and *Pride* Could No Longer put Up with the Battle
Page(s): x

Off we Went with My Ego and Self-delusional *Pride*
Page(s): x

Or Was it Your *Pride*, Pocketbook, Personal Security, or Sex
Page(s): 134

Pride Goeth Before the Fall
Page(s): 133

Self-admiration, Conceit, Abundant Ego are *Pride* Problems
Page(s): 133

Was it Your *Pride*, Pocketbook, Personal Security or Sex Relations
Page(s): 96, 134

Principles

There is No Reason In the World, Not One, to Abandon these *Principles*
Page(s): 53

Problem

A *Problem* That May Not be so Easily Overcome
Page(s): 19

I was My *Problem*
Page(s): 10

If You are Confronted with This *Problem*
Page(s): xv

If You have a *Problem* Regulating Craving's for Sugar
Page(s): 21

Most People Don't Think they Have a *Problem*
Page(s): 20

Now You Understand the *Problem and* the Solution
Page(s): 31

CONCORDANCE   www.bradleyquick.com

www.bradleyquick.com

*Also see Resources Section

Problem's

www.bradleyquick.com

*Also see Resources Section

Process

CONCORDANCE   www.bradleyquick.com

*Also see Resources Section

*Also see Resources Section

*Also see Resources Section

CONCORDANCE www.bradleyquick.com

318

CONCORDANCE

www.bradleyquick.com

*Also see Resources Section

CONCORDANCE

www.bradleyquick.com

While Participating in (Positive Action) Your *Purpose*
Page(s): 118

You Create a *Purpose* in Your Life
Page(s): 129

You have Found a New *Purpose* in Life
Page(s): 54

Your Destination and Your *Purpose*
Page(s): 139

Your Intent and *Purpose* are Pure
Page(s): 29

Q

Quick 10
Page(s): 86

Live *The Quick 10*
Page(s): 82

Read *The Quick 10* Daily
Page(s): 85

Reading *The Quick 10*, and Believing that You Can
Page(s): 83

Quick Fix; also The Quick Fix

A High Level of *The Quick Fix* or Knowledge
Page(s): 132

Allow the *Quick Fix* to Be Your Guide to Freedom
Page(s): 35

DO NOT Postpone Your Participation in the Rest of *The Quick Fix*
Page(s): 83

Fill that Void with this *Quick Fix* Process
Page(s): 123

CONCORDANCE   www.bradleyquick.com

*Also see Resources Section

*Also see Resources Section

R

Radio

Reaction

*Also see Resources Section

Recovery*

Rejection

www.bradleyquick.com

*Also see Resources Section

Relationships

Self-esteem, Ambitions, or Personal *Relationships*?
Page(s): 96, 134

Profound Results in Your Life, *Relationships*, and Goals
Page(s): 65

Your Life and Your *Relationships*
Page(s): 139

Relax

As Your Body and Your Mind Begin to *Relax*
Page(s): 67

As You Focus On *Relaxing* Your Mind
Page(s): 67

As Your Jaw Muscles Begin to *Relax*
Page(s): 68

As Your Lower Neck and Shoulders Begin to *Relax*
Page(s): 68

Attention on Your Mind, and Let it *Relax*
Page(s): 67

Feel Your Upper Neck *Relax*
Page(s): 68

Find a Very Comfortable Place to Sit and *Relax*
Page(s): 66

Hear my Voice as You Start to *Relax*
Page(s): 67

I will Have a Quiet Half-hour All by Myself, and *Relax*
Page(s): 87

I will *Relax* and Trust that The Good I Need will Find Me
Page(s): 94

Just *Relax* and Fall
Page(s): 70

Relief

*Also see Resources Section

Relieve; also Relieved

Hoping to *Relieve* the Pain
Page(s): 58

I was *Relieved* to Say the Least
Page(s): ix

Used Substances to Get up, Lay down, Relax, Sleep, Enhance this, *Relieve* That
Page(s): 137

Religion; see Universe

Remember
Page(s): 51

Remember, All of this Amounts to Our Reactions
Page(s): 79

Remember, Anger is Generally Associated with Fear
Page(s): 121

Remember, Do what You Fear Most and You Control Fear
Page(s): 128

Remember, Earlier I Addressed the Issue of
Page(s): 99

Remember: Easy Does It!
Page(s): 120

Remember, Feelings are Facts, they are Not Truths
Page(s): 131

Remember, for Us, one Drink or one Drug is too Many
Page(s): 39

Remember Honesty Begins with Being Honest with Yourself
Page(s): 124

Remember I Have Value As a Person
Page(s): 133

Remember, if You Can Get Out of Yourself by Being of Service
Page(s): 124

*Also see Resources Section

Remember, if You Keep Doing what You're Doing
Page(s): xvii, 48, 51

Remember, it Works Only if You Work It
Page(s): 134

Remember, it's Easier to Act Yourself into Positive Thinking
Page(s): 57

Remember, it's Not easy Growing Up But it's Well Worth It
Page(s): 39

Remember, it's the Only One You've Got
Page(s): 117

Remember, Listen to or Read this Message
Page(s): 76

Remember, Looking for the Similarities
Page(s): 78

Remember, Muscles have Memory
Page(s): 113

Remember, One is Too Many, a Thousand Not Enough
Page(s): 42

Remember: Positive Action Cures Everything (P.A.C.E.)
Page(s): 32

Remember, Self-doubt is an Illusion
Page(s): 85

Remember, Self Reliance as Far as Any of Us Ever Got
Page(s): 51

Remember Sex is Beautiful if Enjoyed Under the Right Circumstances
Page(s): 137

Remember that Ego, Self-Manifested in Various Ways
Page(s): 125

Remember that I Don't Have to Listen
Page(s): 50

Remember in the Movie there Was a Computer called Hal.
Page(s): 62

*Also see Resources Section

Remember that Never ending Cycle?
Page(s): 39

Remember that Whatever the Emotion or Feeling
Page(s): 80

Remember that You Deserve It
Page(s): 120

Remember, the Best at Anything always Has a Coach
Page(s): 138

Remember, the Closer You Stay to This Process
Page(s): 58

Remember the Tortoise and The Hare?
Page(s): 95

Remember, the Universe and its Inhabitance have Been Around for Millions of Years
Page(s): 118

Remember, There are, From this Point on, No "Big Deals"
Page(s): 88

Remember this Too will Pass It Always Does, and It Always Will
Page(s): 127

Remember to Stretch Before and After Exercise
Page(s): 84

Remember, Today You Have the Ability to Accept
Page(s): 81

Remember, We all Have our Bad Moments
Page(s): 55

Remember, We are Only as Sick As our Secrets
Page(s): 131

Remember, We're in The Efforts Business Not the Results Business
Page(s): xiii

Remember We're Looking for the Similarities
Page(s): 35

Remember Where we Came From
Page(s): 133

*Also see Resources Section

Remember, You can Only Keep what You have by Giving it Away
Page(s): 129

Remember, You Built the Ship You're On
Page(s): 43

Remember, You Had to Work to Learn to Ride a Bike
Page(s): 81

Remember: You're a Winner, so Easy Does It!
Page(s): 37

Remember, You are In the Efforts Business Not the Results Business
Page(s): 33, 84

Remorse; see Guilt

Resentment(s)
Page(s): 96

Resentment a Thought Continuously Resent through The Mind
Page(s): 96, 122

All those You Harbor *Resentments* Towards
Page(s): 97

And You will Achieve Freedom From *Resentments*
Page(s): 96

Be Free of these *Resentments* and Move On
Page(s): 134

Carry those Burdens and *Resentments* Everywhere
Page(s): 89

Expectation is Simply a Premeditated *Resentment*
Page(s): 126

For which You Hold the *Resentment*
Page(s): 126

I Let go of All *Resentments*
Page(s): 94

It Involves *Resentments*
Page(s): 96

*Also see Resources Section

www.bradleyquick.com

*Also see Resources Section

Respond

Response

*Also see Resources Section

Revenge; see Anger

S

Sad

CONCORDANCE

www.bradleyquick.com

*Also see Resources Section

How Many Times in a 24-hour Day are you Happy, *Sad*
Page(s): 78

Mad, Glad, *Sad*, Good or Bad we Must Rely On
Page(s): 35

Scared

This *Scared* Me, I Stopped Drinking and Drugging
Page(s): 11

Maybe Even *Scared* of Doing it Hitting My Knees
Page(s): 15

Second Opinion

Get a *Second Opinion*
Page(s): 88, 135, 136

Secrets

We are Only as Sick as Our *Secrets*
Page(s): 131

You'll Free Yourself from those Issues or *Secrets*
Page(s): 131

Self

Self Acceptance
Page(s): 58

Self Admiration
Page(s): 133

Self Centered
Page(s): 96, 125, 134, 136

Self Confidence
Page(s): 3, 20, 64, 65, 76, 83

Self Containment and Discipline
Page(s): 87

Self Defeating
Page(s): 136

*Also see Resources Section

CONCORDANCE

www.bradleyquick.com

*Also see Resources Section

Self Sabotage

CONCORDANCE   www.bradleyquick.com

Serenity

Serotonin

CONCORDANCE

www.bradleyquick.com

Selective *Serotonin* Reuptake Inhibitors (SSRI's)
Page(s): 21

Serotonin Reuptake Inhibitors
Page(s): 21

Psychedelic Effects by Mimicking *Serotonin*
Page(s): 23

Service; also see Responsibility

Faith, Acceptance, *Service*, and This Too Shall Pass
Page(s): 32, 92, 126

F.A.S.T. *Service*
Page(s): 126

Reaching Out and Being of *Service*
Page(s): 131

Service to Others

Go Be of *Service* to Others
Page(s): 135

How I Can Be of *Service* to Others
Page(s): 127

My willingness To Be of *Service* to Others
Page(s) xi

Positive Change and *Service* to Others
Page(s): xiii

Service to Ourselves and Others
Page(s): 37

Service to Someone
Page(s): 124

Service to Them
Page(s): 127

Sex;* also Sexual
Page(s): 137

A wild *Sex* Addict
Page(s): 5

Decreased *Sexual* Arousal
Page(s): 28

Easy to Escape Through *Sex*
Page(s): 4

Felt Better and Freer with The Opposite *Sex*
Page(s): 13

Is my *Sexual* Relationship Selfish?
Page(s): 137

Sex Can Be a Beautiful Thing
Page(s): 137

Sex Has the Ability to Make us Think
Page(s): 137

Sex is Beautiful if Enjoyed Under the Right Circumstances
Page(s): 137

Sex is One of the Most Powerful Avoidance Mechanisms
Page(s): 137

Sex is Something That all Living Creatures Do
Page(s): 137

The *Sexual* Act is Not to Be Taken Lightly
Page(s): 137

Tried to Have *Sex* with Anyone
Page(s): 4

Visits to *Sex* Shops
Page(s): 10

Was it your Pride, Pocketbook, Personal Security or *Sex* Relations
Page(s): 96, 134

Whether Drugs, *Sex,* Alcohol, Food, Cruising or Money
Page(s): 13

CONCORDANCE www.bradleyquick.com

You will Not Fall Prey to *Sexual* Behavior
Page(s): 137

Shame

Our own Guilt and *Shame*-Based Radio
Page(s): 50

Self-preservation, Self-pity, Deceit, Dishonesty, Guilt or *Shame*
Page(s): 79

Shame and Guilt that Need to Be Processed
Page(s): 112

They are Often Fear or *Shame*-Based
Page(s): 35

Sleep
Page(s): 137

Altered Perceptions, Influenced by Anger, Fear, Lack of Food, *Sleep*
Page(s): 36

At Bedtime Both for Depression and *Sleep* Problems
Page(s): 105

Be the Best you Can Be, through Proper Nutrition, *Sleep*, and
Page(s): 102

Deep *Sleep* . . That's Right… Complete and Total Relaxation
Page(s): 69

Dr. Cass' Nightly CALM™ – for *Sleep*
Page(s): 108

Enough *Sleep* and Daily Exercise is My Answer
Page(s): 101

Getting Ready for *Sleep*
Page(s): 85

Getting the Full Benefit of that *Sleep* Time
Page(s): 102

I Eat Late at Night, After 8 P.m., I Don't *Sleep* Very Well
Page(s): 102

Softer Way

Solution(s)

Somebody

CONCORDANCE

www.bradleyquick.com

Stages; also see Development, Recovery
Page(s): 56

As You Take it Into the Next *Stages* of Your Evolution
Page(s): 58

Let These *Stages*, 1 through 7, Act as Your Guide
Page(s): 58

No time Schedule Associated with These *Stages* of Recovery
Page(s): 58

The Seven *Stages* of Development
Page(s): 56, 133

Stretching; also Stretch
Page(s): 113

Feel this *Stretch* in Your Arms and Shoulders
Page(s): 114

Feel this *Stretch* in your Arm and in Your Chest
Page(s): 114

Hold this *Stretch* for a Count of 20
Page(s): 114

Remember to *Stretch* Before and After Exercise
Page(s): 84

So in *Stretching*, or Opening those Shut Down Muscles
Page(s): 113

Stretch Upper Torso
Page(s): 114

Stretch Lower Torso
Page(s): 113

That's a Full *Stretch* Held for the Appropriate Count
Page(s): 113

The *Stretch* Should Be Felt in the Calf
Page(s): 113

This *Stretch* should Be Felt in the Thigh
Page(s): 114

CONCORDANCE

www.bradleyquick.com

To Do that, You Must Hold the *Stretch*
Page(s): 113

To *Stretch*, Both Before and After Exercise
Page(s): 113

Stuck

Being *Stuck* in Ego
Page(s): 125

I *Stuck* out Like a Sore Thumb
Page(s): 7, 11

I was Alone Again and *Stuck* with Myself
Page(s): xvi

Our Faces Would be *Stuck* to the Ground
Page(s): 115

Stuck in The Problem
Page(s): 37

Sometimes we Get *Stuck* in Isolation
Page(s): 130

We all Have Been *Stuck* in Rush hour Traffic
Page(s): 41

Why Would You Want to Go Hang Out with a *Stuck* Up
Page(s): 125

Subconscious; also see Subconscious Mind

Being in a *Subconscious* State
Page(s): 64, 98

Subconscious Self-sabotage
Page(s): 46

Your Core Beliefs and *Subconscious* Programming
Page(s): 29

Subconscious Mind

Between Your Conscious Mind and *Subconscious Mind*
Page(s): 64

CONCORDANCE www.bradleyquick.com

Substance Abuse*

CONCORDANCE   www.bradleyquick.com

Freedom from Substance Abuse

*Also see Resources Section

Success

Sugar*

CONCORDANCE www.bradleyquick.com

Suggestion

By Altering the Believability and Receptiveness to *Suggestion*
Page(s): 63

My *Suggestion* Is

My *Suggestion* Is you Eat only Fresh and Whole Foods
Page(s): 100

My *Suggestion* Is you Make this Part of Your *Daily Journal* Activity
Page(s): 96

My *Suggestion* Is you Eat only Fresh and Whole Foods
Page(s): 100

My *Suggestion* Is to stay away from all those preservatives
Page(s): 100

Suicide*

Found in Those with: Depression, Anxiety, *Suicide*, Violence
Page(s): 23

You Can Commit *Suicide*, We've All thought About It
Page(s): 43

Supplements

Holistic Formula *Supplements*
Page(s): 106, 108, 109, 110, 112

Surrender (I give up)
Page(s): 57

I Was Always Ready to *Surrender* My Will (what I want)
Page(s): xvi

With this *Surrender* Comes a Newfound Freedom
Page(s): 57

Why Would You Not *Surrender* to the Cure?
Page(s): 56

T

Task
Page(s): 139

All You Can do is the *Task* at Hand
Page(s): 139

Better Results with Daily Efforts in Regards to this *Task*
Page(s): 95

He Didn't Have to Think About what *Task* he Was to Do Next
Page(s): 84

I Just Do the Next *Task* on My Schedule
Page(s): 84

Participating in a *Task* or Just Listening to Another's Problems
Page(s): 127

This *Task* will Optimize Your Hard Drive
Page(s): 91

Wherever that Path May Lead, My *Task* is to Follow It
Page(s): 17

Today: also see Just for Today

Acceptance is The Key to All of Our Problems *Today*
Page(s): 56

Adult onset Diabetes is Epidemic *Today*
Page(s): 24

It Remains True *Today*
Page(s): 128

Just This Moment, *Today*
Page(s): 38

Learned Through Your Experience *Today*
Page(s): 85

Let's Begin to Fix It *Today*
Page(s): 32

CONCORDANCE www.bradleyquick.com

*Also see Resources Section

*Also see Resources Section

Today I Release the Fear
Page(s): 72, 94

Today I Let Go of Resentments
Page(s): 72

Today I Acknowledge My Fear and Anxiety
Page(s): 73

Today I Am Responsible
Page(s): 72, 94

Today I Have Enough Time
Page(s): 73

Today You Have the Ability to Accept
Page(s): 81

Today I have The Ability to Say "No"
Page(s): 94

Today I'm Finding the Willingness
Page(s): 129

Today, I'm the Best Me I've Ever Been
Page(s): 54

Today I Let Go of Painful Experiences
Page(s): 73, 94

Today I Open My Heart
Page(s): 73, 94

Today I See Beyond My Fear
Page(s): 72, 94

Today I Walk Through My Fear
Page(s): 73

Today, Just Do the Job That's Put in Front of You
Page(s): 84

Today, Stay Out of Self-pity
Page(s): 84

Tomorrow Will Be a Better Day than *Today*
Page(s): 85

www.bradleyquick.com   CONCORDANCE

Tolerance

Tomorrow

CONCORDANCE   www.bradleyquick.com

CONCORDANCE www.bradleyquick.com

Trust

CONCORDANCE   www.bradleyquick.com

*Also see Resources Section

You can *Trust* and Have Faith in this Process
Page(s): 43

U

Uncover Discover and Discard

How to *Uncover, Discover and Discard*
Page(s): 91

Uncover, Discover and Discard what You Think you Know
Page(s): xiii

Willing to *Uncover, Discover and Discard* the Past
Page(s): 118

Unhappy

Unhappy, Sorry, Dejected, Depressed
Page(s): 135

Unintentional

The *Unintentional* Defeating of Your Own best Interests
Page(s): 29

Unique Identifying Factors

Every One of us Has *Unique Identifying Factors*
Page(s): 117

Universe

A Perfect Part of This *Universe*
Page(s): 120

A Sincere Request to the *Universe*
Page(s): 16

Being at One with The World and The *Universe*
Page(s): 138

CONCORDANCE

www.bradleyquick.com

CONCORDANCE   www.bradleyquick.com

www.bradleyquick.com

*Also see Resources Section

*Also see Resources Section

V

Vitamins

CONCORDANCE

www.bradleyquick.com

*Also see Resources Section

Weight*

Willing; also see Willingness

CONCORDANCE

www.bradleyquick.com

CONCORDANCE www.bradleyquick.com

Willingness

World; also see Planet

CONCORDANCE

www.bradleyquick.com

*Also see Resources Section

www.bradleyquick.com

*Also see Resources Section

*Also see Resources Section

*Also see Resources Section

www.bradleyquick.com

CONCORDANCE   www.bradleyquick.com

List *Your Part*
Page(s): 96, 134

You Must then List *Your Part*
Page(s): 96, 134

Look at *Your Part*
Page(s): 137

Your Disorders; see Our Disorders

CONCORDANCE

www.bradleyquick.com

24-Hour Alcohol and Drug Help Line
(800)448-3000

24-Hour National Depression Hotline
(800) 242-2211

24-Hour Suicide Hotline
(800) 784-2433
http://www.suicidehotline.com

Al-Anon/Alateen Family Group Headquarters, Inc.
P.O. Box 862
Midtown Station
New York, NY 10018-0862
(800) 344-2666
http://www.al-anon.alateen.org

Alcoholics Anonymous (AA) World Services, Inc.
475 Riverside Drive
New York, NY 10015
(212) 870-3400

American Council for Drug Education
204 Monroe Street, Suite 110
Rockville, MD 20850
(800) 488-3784

American Medical Association
http://www.well.com/user/woa/woarollo.htm

American Meditation Institute for
Yoga Science and Philosophy
60 Garner Road
Averill Park, NY 12018
http://www.americanmeditation.org

Anxiety Disorders Association of America
http://www.adaa.org

Be Totally Free!
A true solution for emotional eating, eating disorders, weight
loss and addictions. (310) 281-8831
www.betotallyfree.com

Boys and Girls Clubs of America
1230 West Peachtree Street, NW
Atlanta, GA 30309
(404) 815-5766
www.bgca.org

Big Brothers and Big Sisters of America
(215) 567-7000

Center for Loss and Life Transition
For books related to children and grief
Fort Collins, CO
(970) 226-6050
http://www.centerforloss.com

Center for Substance Abuse Treatment
(800) 662-HELP

Center for Substance Abuse Prevention
(800) WORKPLACE

Change Your Water, Change Your Life!
Aging is a loss of Hexagonal Water
from organs, tissues and cells, and an
overall decrease in total body water.
Replenishing the Hexagonal Water in
our bodies can increase vitality, slow
the aging process, and prevent disease
http://www.TheQuickFixWater.com

Children of Alcoholics Foundation, Inc.
Box 4185
Grand Central Station
New York, NY 10115
(800) 359-2633

Cocaine Anonymous (CA)
3740 Overland Avenue, Suite G
Los Angeles, CA 90034
(800)347-8998
(310 559-5833
www.ca.org

**Community AntiDrug
Coalitions of America (CADCA)**
625 Slaters Lane, Suite 300
Alexandria, VA 22314
(800) 54CADCA, ext. 242
www.cadca.org

**The Cool Change Foundation, Inc.
Successful Processes For Positive Life Change**
P.O. Box 160
North Hollywood, CA 91603
(800) 329-0474
www.TheCoolChangeFoundation.org

Debtors Anonymous
P.O. Box 920888
Needham, MA 02492-0009
(781) 453-2743
www.debtorsanonymous.org

Eating Disorders Awareness and Prevention
http://www.nationaleatingdisorders .com

Emotions Anonymous International
PO Box 4245
St. Paul, MN 55104-0245
(651) 647-9712
www.emotionsanonymous.org

Gamblers Anonymous
International Service Office
P.O. Box 17173
Los Angeles, CA 90017
(213) 386-8789
www.isomain@gamblersanonymous.org

Gambling Treatment Services in Eastern Missouri
Bridgeway Counseling Services, Inc.
1601 Old S. River Rd.
St. Charles, MO 63303
(636) 949-9940
razer@ix.netcom.com

Grief Recovery Institute
Help line (800) 445-4808
http://www.grief-recovery.com

Hazelden Information Center
Addiction treatment, publishing, education,
research, and recovery support
CO 3, PO Box 11
Center City, MN 55012 0011
(800) 257-7810
http://www.hazelden.org

Holistic Technologies
Donna Eckwortzel
Holistic Health Techniques
Boost Immunity - Reverse Aging
(916) 521-1343
www.measurethedifference.com

ICFDA
International Coalition For Drug Awareness
http://www.drugawareness.org/

Join Together
Advancing Effective Alcohol and
Drug Policy, Prevention, and Treatment
One Appleton Street, 4th Floor
Boston, MA 02116-5223
(617) 437-1500
www.jointogether.org

The Johnson Institute
613 Second St. N.E.
Washington, D.C. 20002
(202) 662-7104
www.johnsoninstitute.com

Kriya Yoga Institute
http://kriya.org/

www.bradleyquick.com

Marijuana Anonymous
P.O. Box 2912
Van Nuys, CA 91404
(800) 766-6779
info@marijuanaanonymous.org

Moderation Management Network, Inc.
PO Box 6005
Ann Arbor, Michigan 48106
(313) 677-6007

NarAnon Family Groups
P.O. Box 2562
Palos Verdes Peninsula, CA 90274
(310) 547-5800

Narconon International
Drug Prevention and Rehabilitation Services
Phone: (323) 962-2404
Toll Free: (800) 468-6933
Website: www.narconon.org
Email: info@narconon.org

Narcotics Anonymous (NA) World Services
P.O. Box 9999
Van Nuys, CA 91409
(800) 863-2962
(818) 780-3951

National Association for Children of Alcoholics
11426 Rockville Pike, Suite 100
Rockville, MD 20852
(301) 468-0985

National Association Iyengar Yoga
3940 Laurel Canyon Blvd #947
Studio City , CA 91604
(800) 889-9642
http://www.iynaus.org/

National Clearinghouse for Alcohol and Drug Information
P.O. Box 2345
Rockville, MD 20847-2345
(800) 729-6686
http://www.health.org

National Council on Alcoholism and Drug Dependence (NCADD)
12 West 21st Street
New York, NY 10010
(800) 622-2255

National Depressive and Manic Depressive Association
http://www.mnda.org

National Families in Action
2296 Henderson Mill Road Ste 204
Atlanta, GA 30345
(404) 934-6364
http://www.emory.edu/NFIA/

National Federation of Parents for DrugFree Youth
1820 Franwell Avenue, Suite 16
Silver Spring, MD 20902
(301) 649-7100

National Inhalant Prevention Coalition
1201 W. Sixth Street, Ste. C200
Austin, TX 78703
(800) 269-4237
(512) 480-8953

National Institute on Drug Abuse (NIDA)
5600 Fishers Lane, Room 10A39
Rockville, MD 20902
(301) 649-7100

www.bradleyquick.com

R E S O U R C E S www.bradleyquick.com

Nicotine Anonymous World Services
419 Main St.
PO Box #370
Huntington Beach, CA 92648
(415) 750-0328
http://nicotineanonymous.org
info@nicotineanonymous.org

Overeaters Anonymous World Services
POB 44020
Rio Rancho, NM 87124
(505) 891-2664
www.overeatersanonymous.org

Phoenix House Foundation's National Helpline
(800) 662-4357
www.drughelp.org

Prozac: Panacea or Pandora?
Dr. Ann Blake Tracy - Author
P.O. Box 1044
West Jordan, UT 84084
(800) 280-0730
http://members.aol.com/atracyphd/

S.A.V.E.
Stop Antidepressant Violence from Escalating
http://www.thesaveproject.com/

Sexaholics Anonymous
PO Box 3565
Brentwood, TN 37024
(866) 424-8777
Saico@sa.org

Sexual Compulsives Anonymous International
PO Box 1585
Old Chelsea Station
New York, NY 10011
(212) 439-1123

Sex and Love Addicts Anonymous
PO Box 338
Norwood, MA 02062-0338
(781) 255-8825
www.slaafws.org

The Way to Happiness
A Common Sense Guide to Better Living
(818) 254-0600
www.twth.org

Workaholics Anonymous
World Service Organization
P.O. Box 289
Menlo Park, CA 94026-0289
(510) 273-9253 or (800)-622-2255
wso@workaholicsanonymous.org
www.workaholicsanonymous.org

www.bradleyquick.com

TUESDAY

WEDNESDAY

DAILY JOURNAL

www.bradleyquick.com

THURSDAY

FRIDAY

SATURDAY

Cut Out and Keep it with you to remember
The Quick 10.

The Quick 10

Just for Today I will try to live through this day only, one moment at a time, and not try to tackle all my problems at once. I'm capable of doing something for a few hours that would appall me if I thought I had to keep it up for a lifetime.

So I certainly can live in, and for, today.

Just for Today I will be happy. Abraham Lincoln once said that "Most folks are as happy as they make up their minds to be." Today I have made up my mind to be happy!

Just for Today I will alter myself to what is and not try to adjust everything to fit my own desires. I will take life as it comes and fit myself to it.

Just for Today I will try to strengthen my body and mind. I will study something useful and I will exercise. I will not be a mental loafer or a coach potato. I will do something that requires effort, thought and concentration.

Just for Today I will exercise my soul in three ways: I will do someone a good turn and not tell anyone about it. If anyone knows of it, it will not count. I will do at least a couple of things I don't want to do, just for good measure.

I will not show anyone that my feelings are hurt. They may be hurt, but today I will not show it.

Just for Today I will be agreeable. I will look as well as I can, dress becomingly, keep my voice low, be courteous and criticize not one bit. I won't find fault with anything, nor try to improve or regulate anybody but myself.

Just for Today I will work this process. I may not follow it exactly, but I will work it. I will save myself from two pests: *Hurry and Indecision.*

Just for Today I will have a quiet halfhour all by myself, and relax. During this halfhour I will try to get a better perspective of my life.

Just for Today I will be unafraid. I will especially not be afraid to enjoy what is beautiful and to believe that as *I give to the world, so the world will give to me.*

Just for Today I will put my best efforts forward in all I do I will stay out of the results and acknowledge that today I am in the efforts business not the results business.